The art of being unhappy

Dr. Nelio Tombini

The art of being unhappy

Disarming emotional traps

With a foreword by J. J. Camargo

The art of being unhappy

The contents of this book are the sole responsibility of the author and do not necessarily reflect the views of the publisher.

ISBN: 978-1-64095-658-2
Ebook ISBN: 978-1-64095-659-9

Editorial production and distribution:

contato@citadel.com.br
www.citadel.com.br

Distributed in English language by:

SOUND WISDOM
P.O. Box 310 • Shippensburg, PA 17257-0310 • 717-530-2122
info@soundwisdom.com

I would like to thank the patients who trusted me, to the extent that they shared their secrets and sufferings with me. In this way, they have helped me to become more intimate and perceptive about emotional life and its insides. A special thank you to the SUS patients at Santa Casa de Porto Alegre. For 25 years, we have grown together through weekly group psychotherapy sessions. I learned a lot about psychological suffering and the solutions sought by people with many limitations in life.

To my friends Alexandre Mota, Adelino Cruz, Alexandre Godinho, Rogério Gil and Mateus Colombo Mendes, who encouraged me and accompanied me in the task of writing the book. Finally, to Dr. J. J. Camargo, whom I have admired since I was his student, for his willingness to write the preface to this book.

Summary

FOREWORD
by J. J. Camargo

Nelio Tombini is a restless soul. It was probably this restlessness that pushed him into psychiatry, with its endless challenges - some decipherable and others not so much - regarding this mysterious compartment that is the human mind. Beloved by his patients and respected by his peers, Nelio has reached a level of professional stability that would usually satisfy ordinary souls, but not the restless ones.

Driven by an uncontainable desire to share what he had gleaned over almost 40 years in psychiatry, he decided to create communication channels that would bring his specialty to the general public. He began by recording a series of videos which, in an interactive and accessible way, discussed personal reactions and attitudes to everyday provocations.

Probably stimulated by the success of this initiative - and dissatisfied because he is the kind of person who gets into trouble with routine, since he believes that a life that justifies itself imposes a continuous expansion of limits - he embarked on this ambitious project of transferring his rich psychoanalytic experiences to the eager pages of a textbook. And the accounts are so fluent and the language so uncomplicated that we often feel like we're at the patient's bedside, like improvised participants in the treatment, because we understand the subject.

Soon afterwards, we find ourselves surprised and, suspicious, we look at the couch with sympathy, as if the text had been written for us, on demand, throwing us into the role of patients, after our period of pride as amateur therapists.

It's impressive to see the wealth of people who have somehow built up their unhappiness. Seen from the outside, the situations seem invariably predictable, although the protagonists don't realize it, busy as they are with denial (as a simplistic solution) or shifting the blame (as an escape route).

Guilt, such a bitter and exhausting feeling, is dissected in depth in this book, revealing the most varied circumstances in which it impregnated the victim's spirit, leading to depression and all its consequences, of which suicide is obviously the most fearsome.

Exaggerated demands - at work, in social life, in marriage - end up building an implacable monster that governs the victim's behavior, trapped in a world of bitterness and suffering. When unmasked in therapy, they illustrate how much we suffer from fanciful and unfair stereotypes.

In the management of some depressive conditions, the low efficacy of chemical therapy and the decisive participation of the word, the basic tool of psychoanalysis, is elegantly argued when the patient, frightened and needy, knocks on the door with an explicit cry for help.

Going through the pages of this book made me understand Nelio's enthusiasm for publishing it. Anyone who writes knows when what they've written is consistent, and that feeling is rightly euphoric for the author.

As I scrolled page by page on the monitor, I missed the conventional, printed model of the book - the one you are now handling with curiosity. It would have solved my repeated desire to hug it, but then I ran into the affective rigidity of the computer, which is not very fond of intimacy.

No one should claim to be an expert by the end of this book. However, there is no doubt that this dive into the human soul will make each reader a more understanding, sweet and generous person. Embrace it.

J. J. CAMARGO

José de Jesus Peixoto Camargo is a surgeon who graduated from UFRGS and did postgraduate studies at the Mayo Clinic in Minnesota, USA. A pioneer in lung transplantation in Latin America, Camargo also performed the first double lung transplant in Brazil.

PRESENTATION

Emotional Illiteracy and the art of being unhappy

by Dr. Nelio Tombini

First of all, I'd like to remind you that I'm a psychiatrist, not a writer or journalist. I say this so that you have tolerance and patience for my way of writing, without great linguistic refinement.

This book is the result of various actions that I have developed throughout my life. I have always had a concern and a desire to share my perceptions and knowledge about the workings of the unconscious, the psyche and the emotional with the lay public.

I worked in community centers, health centers and also at Santa Casa de Porto Alegre, where we created the Affective Disorders Service three decades ago. As well as outpatient care, we focused on group psychotherapy for patients on the Unified Health System. Finally, in 1992, I created Psicobreve - Clínica de Psicoterapias Breves, formed by a group of psychiatrists and psychologists.

Adapting this desire to share knowledge with the general public to current technologies, I created a psycho-educational project using a series of videos called "5 minutes with psychiatrist Nelio Tombini", published on YouTube and Facebook.* I also give talks, *workshops* and consultancies to organizations, groups and companies, trying to help them manage emotional issues and their impact on their personal and professional lives.

The intention of this book is one: to offer the reader ways of understanding our intricate and complex unconscious (or psyche). By developing these insights, we will probably have a better chance of not falling into **emotional traps** - created by ourselves or by others. As we enter these traps, by choice or connivance, we complicate our lives, making them so difficult that we don't enjoy them. Some people go down this rocky path and become *experts* in the construction of suffering, becoming specialists in what I call the **art of being unhappy**.

---

* Facebook: facebook.com/drneliotombini; Instagram: instagram.com/drneliotombini; YouTube: youtube.com/use/Psicobreve; Twitter: twitter.com/dr_neliotombini.

If readers are interested in the psychic world, they will find several articles here that will allow them to develop a more intimate understanding of these issues and of what we call the soul. My desire is to share experiences, to share stories I've seen in everyday life and to show the repercussions of emotional conflicts on each of us and on life in general.

I believe that it is possible to transfer understandings and concepts about psychic life, even outside the offices of psychiatrists and psychologists. In other words, everyone can understand subjective emotional manifestations and the damage they can cause. That was my aim in offering the videos and the interactions on social networks, complemented by this book in a deeper and more consistent way.

I realize that people tend to deny the existence of the internal, emotional or psychic world. Without this intimacy with the emotional, we will suffer damage to our well-being, our ability to relate, the development of creativity, love relationships and the success of our lives.

I offer an abstraction to help you better understand our daily lives. Let's say that life is built on two pillars: one comprises intelligence, knowledge, culture and academic training; the other represents emotional or psychic life. The column that most influences daily life is the one that supports the emotional. This can even lead to transformations in the intellectual. The column that supports the intellectual, objective knowledge, can bring little benefit to the psychic side.

Unfortunately, institutions and even individuals invest more in intellectual development, not least because it's easier and more accessible. Look at the number of books, *websites*, apps, television programs and everything else that exists to help us take care of our physical health. We learn about everything, look for the best methods, apply them to ourselves and share them with others.

On the other hand, the information offered in the media and in public policies aimed at the prevention and development of mental health is poor and scarce. Institutions, organizations and companies in general invest little or nothing in the emotional development of their employees. However, they do spend a considerable amount of money on courses and training related to technical knowledge, with which they imagine they can leverage the organization's growth and turnover.

In this context, the emotional, which is the flagship of our lives, is forgotten. If there are investments aimed at changing the way people act and relate to each other, they are limited to the world of self-help, which provides practical tips for changing behavior, in an attempt to make changes from the outside in, but little is known about the actual results.

Although neglected, emotional issues control all other areas of life. Many prejudices about mental suffering need to be eliminated. For example, it is very uncommon for us to arrive at work and openly tell our colleagues that we are depressed, anxious, sleepless or having family conflicts. We don't talk or expose ourselves, because we understand that talking about mental suffering is a sign of weakness. However, we do speak out when we suffer from migraines, premenstrual tension, renal colic, asthma, gluten intolerance, etc. It's hard to live like this, hiding what really makes us suffer.

It is because of these observations that I present this book, to stimulate your reflections and, at the same time, suggest ways to change. The idea is that we can use new tools to alleviate the afflictions of the soul and the psychic symptoms that result from them.

I once published an article in the Porto Alegre newspaper Zero Hora, with a very suggestive title: "Emotional illiterates". The text had a lot to do with this book, as it warned about how little we know about our psychic apparatus. The knowledge we have of these aspects is generally flawed, untrained and insufficient. I call it the **psychic apparatus** because I compare it to other systems we are used to - the digestive system, the circulatory system and others.

All these systems need to work well for life to develop for longer and with greater quality. From an emotional point of view, we are at least semi-literate - if not completely so. Don't be offended by this language, it's not a demerit for the readers. It's a strong force of expression, used to get your attention.

The thing is, there is no culture that refers to or encourages us to think about the way we work, our personality, our emotions. In schools, for example, we don't talk about these subjects. At most, there is some discussion about sexuality. Nor is it common within the family to look at the other, to observe how the other expresses themselves, reacts, what they feel and how they relate. Basically, we relate intuitively. Some may be lucky enough to be born into a family group with healthier, more respectful, more sensitive and perceptive parents, who are able to be more intimate with their own emotional life and that of their children. That's great! But this is certainly the exception, not the rule.

I remember my family experience. A family of Italian origin, living in the interior of Rio Grande do Sul, in a small town. At home, and even at school, there was no habit of reading. My parents' relationship with their children was all about general care and conferencing. No more intimate conversations. The bond was based on demands when chores weren't done or when attitudes were inappropriate. However, I consider my parents to be good people; they didn't cause us any emotional damage and they did what they could.

Many of our readers have had parents or family members who are very psychologically compromised. The presence of mental illness in parents causes serious psychological damage to their children. Imagine parents with depression, alcoholism, abusive, suspicious, aggressive, overly rigid and other unhealthy characteristics. How many scars remain in their children's lives? It's also important to think about the conditions of poverty and limitations of all kinds that many people have faced in their lives, causing emotional illness.

Today's technological times also don't help us with the task of saying what we think, what we feel. Today, people are more distant from each other, despite the great facilities of virtual communication. Everyone knows about everyone else's life, but in a very superficial way. No intimacy. On the internet, everything smells of *fake*, falsehood, make-believe and appearances. Pleasure is sought frantically and must come immediately, even if alcohol or other drugs are used to achieve it.

In relationships between couples, affection, care and complicity can wait. Urgency only exists in sex life. This comes first; other affections are not treated as relevant - perhaps there isn't even time to find out if they would be present in the relationship. Of course, it's fine if people prioritize sex at any time they want - but the relationship can become impoverished and empty if this is the only point of contact and interest between those involved.

As we don't realize the harm caused by emotional maladjustments, we run the risk of medicating patients in an unreasonable way, with the fantasy of fighting the ills of the soul with medication. I'm not disqualifying psychiatric medication, which, if properly applied, has satisfactory results and benefits many people. However, I notice that all medical specialties prescribe psychotropic drugs when faced with any expression of psychological suffering. Even psychiatrists tend to medicate before even listening to the problems of the mind.

If it's hard enough to find comfort in a doctor's office, it's even harder to find it in specialized literature. If we look for books that talk about emotional or psychic life, we'll find a large number, but with language that is often unintelligible to the lay public. They are subjective, theoretical, dry publications, more aimed at the academic world.

All that said, I'm here to make progress in this field that is as important as it is neglected, which is emotional life. That's why I'm offering this book in simple, clear, accessible, understandable and direct language. I hope and expect that, after reading this book, readers will be equipped and empowered to make their daily lives more interesting, less conflictual and less painful.

The reflections here are permeated with examples and situations that I have experienced myself, showing that I have the same difficulties in life as the readers. However, when faced with everyday conflicts or raids, I am perhaps more agile in finding a solution that is more harmonious for my emotions and for facing the reality that surrounds me - simply because I am always very attentive to these issues. And it is to this advance that I invite readers.

In addition to the book, there are other approaches that can help bring about change. Psychotherapy can give your life a ***boost***. They can be brief or focused, objective and quick. Freud already used these more dynamic approaches with his patients, which could take up to twenty sessions. They can also be longer, like psychoanalysis.

Psychological counseling works like a *start* or a trigger. It can take place in occasional meetings and helps the person to rethink certain actions in their daily life, at work or with their family. The other day, in a bookstore, I met a lady who asked if I was Nelio Tombini. I said yes, but that I didn't remember her. She told me that she had talked to me once and that I had helped her solve her problem during that single meeting. I thought about it and asked what I had said that was so wonderful and profound. When she told me what I had said, I was surprised, because it was something very simple that a friend could have said. Perhaps, as it was spoken by a mental health professional, it was taken more seriously, giving better results.

Reading, lectures, *workshops* and even more intimate and frank conversations with friends can also help.

I hope you don't consider me pretentious, but we can get rid of the **art of being unhappy** and try to have a more interesting, more satisfying life, with fewer conflicts and, consequently, more pleasure.

Day after day, without realizing it, without wanting to, without knowing it,
we strive in an ancient art - the art of being unhappy.
In the decisions we make, in what we say,
in the way we feel, in almost everything,
almost always, we act against ourselves.
The bad news is that, even if we learn to
control these impulses of our psyche, they
will always be there, ready to act as soon as we get careless.
But the good - the excellent - news is that there is,
many ways to control our natural instincts
that lead us to unhappiness.
That's what I've been working on for decades.
And that's what I'm sharing with you here.

CARELESSNESS WITH WORDS

Verbal communication is fundamental to understanding between living beings, especially between humans. Words have power. They can start relationships or end them. We should definitely think again before offering our words to someone, especially when we give them in the form of an opinion.

Perhaps the most frequent abuse we commit in human relationships is verbal. We often say the wrong thing out of irritation, impatience or disinterest. It's something that escapes us very easily. It worries me when we speak to someone we're intimate with, someone we like, whose respect should be reciprocated, but we end up being offensive.

Verbal exaggeration is understandable when we're fighting, or even when we're talking to someone we don't have good feelings for. Of course, even in these cases we have to be careful with our words. However, we don't realize that we are often even more cruel to people who are close and dear to us.

Look around you. Notice your relationships and those of others. A father speaks rudely to his children. They do the same to their mother. A boyfriend berates his girlfriend; a teacher berates a student, who in turn offends him. It's not uncommon to see swearing, shouting and threats instead of sober, respectful conversations. Often, this verbal abuse takes place ironically, as if the abuse were justified.

This happens precisely because we allow ourselves to speak our minds to those close to us. It should be the other way around! It's not because we are close to someone that we can mistreat them. Instead, we should exercise the utmost care in our choice of words. In conversations, when we offer a thought to the other person, it is assumed that the exchange of opinions is free. But that doesn't give anyone permission to say everything that comes to mind.

Nor should we forget another form of verbal abuse: uncontrolled chatter. There are people who talk all the time, on any subject, regardless of whether or not the other person is interested in the conversation. It's as if they were talking to themselves. This behavior makes the other person disinterested and want to distance themselves. Since it's usually impossible to physically distance oneself from the interlocutor, the bored listener distances themselves mentally, taking their thoughts to distant places and not paying the slightest attention to the speaker. And so relationships become more superficial and damaging.

Care with words needs to be developed in everyone. I think the best school to learn this is childhood. That's why parents need to be careful how they speak to their children. There is a clear downgrading of the relationship with children. It used to be common for parents to say things to their children like:

"That's grown-up talk. Don't bother."

"Don't go where you're not wanted."

"Get out of here and go play!"

"What you think doesn't matter in the slightest."

These approaches can result in an adult who will verbally abuse or allow themselves to be abused. Nowadays, children have acquired a special power and tend to abuse their parents.

* * *

Being intelligent, cultured, having a university degree, money or power, none of this guarantees that a person has the gift of taking care of the content and form of their conversations. What makes the difference is the perception and sensitivity of what can and cannot be offered to the other person. Having this filter between what we think and what we say is the real difference.

Does it sound difficult? It is difficult! If we don't pay attention to these premises, the person listening to us won't pay attention to us, won't consider our opinion to be relevant. They may also become irritated or hurt and respond harshly, raising the tone of the conversation even higher.

All this may seem silly, precisely because what we do most in life is talk and talk. However, taking care of what we say and how we say it is fundamental

- for us and for others. It's obvious that at some point we lose our temper, shouting, swearing or even physically attacking someone. I myself, by virtue of my profession, say very harsh things to my patients, which are necessary for the therapy to run smoothly. This is also because my aim is to convey what I perceive and think with tenderness. On the other hand, I always try to see if it makes sense and if it will be beneficial for the patient.

For a reflection exercise, I've listed some examples of verbal abuse. Think about what you've witnessed, heard or even said.

The person goes on a diet, loses weight and becomes slender. They meet a friend who, instead of complimenting them, asks: "Did you get AIDS?"

Another has hair implants, and his friend tells him: "That's not a man's thing!"

The woman is happy with her new boyfriend and meets a friend, who comments: "That guy doesn't suit you."

Friends meet and one says to the other: "You should dye your hair."

A real case: a friend of mine, culturally and professionally distinguished, who considers me to be a good professional, introduced me to an acquaintance of his, saying: "This is Nélio Tombini, a psychiatrist who's a bit crazy."

So let's pay attention to verbal abuse, the source of so many disagreements, resentments and estrangement. Sometimes we forget the power of speech, the strength of words - which can be devastating or redeeming, depending on what and how we say them.

Obviously, I don't want to disqualify or minimize the other abuses that occur in human relationships.

By the way, do you know how bullying differs from the abuse I'm talking about? Bullying is intentional physical or emotional violence. **Verbal abuse** is emotional violence, but it's unconscious, which makes it more difficult to perceive and even take a stand against.

An important tip for dealing with these situations: tell the abuser that you didn't like the way he expressed himself. Telling the truth usually relieves us, because we won't go home with the upset stuck in our throats.

I also include in the list of verbal abuses this style of relationship that is present in our daily lives: what **we think**. People say what they think about everything all the time, even if they have no idea about the subject. This is how virtual media works.

Finally, let's be aware of the abusers' strategy of softening their verbal aggression. They often say something like: "It was a joke, don't get upset..." Well, let's get upset! And be careful not to upset others.

OBSTACLES IN LOVE RELATIONSHIPS

Throughout history, many things have changed in human relations. Social, labor and family dynamics have changed as societies have changed. In the past, people usually got together for family, economic and political reasons. Love bonds were not taken into account at these times. Of course, men and women cherished them, but they were not taken into account when choosing partners. However, one thing has essentially never changed: we are always looking for a loving relationship. Someone who completes us, who admires us, who arouses our desire, with whom it's good to talk, have sex, go for a walk. This is a constant human quest.

Considering the motto of this book, that we are experts in sabotaging ourselves, in keeping ourselves from happiness, and taking into account all the years of professional observations, I can say that this search is not easy at all, nor does it have well-established rules.

In our eagerness to find happiness with - and through - a person, we can be afflicted with loneliness, running the risk of subjecting ourselves to situations of discomfort, inconvenience, suffering and unhappiness. Often, we don't even really know what we're looking for in a relationship, but what stands out, what attracts and seduces us the most, is usually the appearance of the person we've chosen or the power they wield. Of course, let's not forget the possibility of idealizing the object of desire. In this case, the risk of a failed relationship is very high.

Well, first of all, we have a very common feature in today's relationships: the body, physical, sexual issue. This in itself is not a problem. Intimate relationships are, in fact, an unequivocal source of pleasure. The problem here is not the essence, but how it is used. Today, many relationships begin and are sustained exclusively on the basis of sex.

It's understandable that physical attraction is the impetus for getting closer, but if that's all there is, the affair will inevitably run out of steam. It won't be long before one of the partners looks elsewhere for the stimulus that brought them closer to the person with whom they are already dissatisfied. And they will do so after breaking up, or even while the relationship is still ongoing. This explains why most relationships that revolve around "chemistry" and attraction end up leaving great traumas in one of the people involved. It's a constant leaving and being left, stimulated by an emptiness that one seeks to fill with another attractive body, generating more emptiness.

Women's sex lives have changed a lot, for the better, since the advent of the contraceptive pill. The door has been opened to sexual pleasure without the risk of pregnancy. Women were allowed to have sex with more partners before marriage. Nowadays, it seems that they are embarking on a second sexual revolution, having sex even without much love or affection for their partner. What was already being enjoyed by men is now also being enjoyed by women. They go out with a man the day or night they meet him just to enjoy the pleasures of the alcove, of sex. Social media such as Facebook, WhatsApp and dating *sites* have facilitated these encounters, which are more focused on the exchange of carnal pleasures.

I think it's very good and healthy to look for relationships in which attraction is a considerable factor, but it's important that we know exactly what we're looking for in a relationship. That women and men want, respectively, "princes" and "princesses" to show off in the street and "alpha males" and "libertines" to enjoy intimately is reasonable and understandable.

Furthermore, looking for a powerful man, an imposing woman, wealthy, socially well-connected partners who attract attention in society and please everyone's eyes is no guarantee of anything in terms of relationships. This kind of search can hide a subliminal, unconscious desire to find someone to take care of us, to take us in, to take charge of our lives. This can be a big mistake, because no one but ourselves is capable of taking charge of our lives. In fact, when someone approaches us with the intention of looking after and protecting us, the best thing to do is run away! Because, in the end, we really will be subjected to this person, and what at first seemed like a good idea, due to a fantasy of redemption, could bring a lot of suffering. As the saying goes, "there's no such thing as a free lunch". Then comes the bill.

Well, these can be some of the stumbling blocks that arise at the beginning of relationships - or even before, when we're still flirting, getting closer. What I usually offer for reflection to those who suffer from the consequences of poorly established relationships and who want something more intimate and consistent is that, first of all, they should know what they're looking for. Don't be embarrassed to be able to tell someone who just wants to have sex that this kind of relationship doesn't interest you. People who want more than sex, but allow themselves to have sex for the sake of momentary sexual pleasure, often fall into a void when the emotions of orgasm are over. Women often find it difficult to refuse a furtive invitation to have sex, because they imagine that refusing could permanently alienate their partner's interest in continuing the relationship.

Perhaps the best way to really get to know someone is to talk to them. It's difficult to do this at night, as there's often a lot of noise pollution. You need time and the ability to listen carefully to what the other person is offering you and informing you. If you want to know how someone thinks and acts, it's simple: let them talk. It sounds easy, but it isn't.

The art of listening, elaborating, keeping quiet and giving back to the other person in an appropriate and delicate way is more difficult than it seems. If we want intimacy, complicity and closeness with someone, we will necessarily have to tell them what we think, who we are, our interests, desires, tastes and plans. Of course, I'm also referring to plans for our affective and love lives.

It sounds silly. "Well, who doesn't talk about themselves?" you might be asking yourself. True, there is no one who doesn't talk about themselves, but in the early stages, it's common for people to create characters for themselves, or embellish their characteristics a little, in order to please and win over a potential partner. So it's essential that we tell the absolute truth about ourselves. In the long run, we prefer that the person we're with stays that way because they liked the real personality they met, not a projection or performance.

In the same way, we must try to listen openly to the person with whom we are beginning to have a relationship, openly. What do they really think, want, like, dislike, do and don't do? What can we expect from them? From what I observe, people talk a lot about what they do, what they have, how happy they are, how much money they have, the trips they take. But they say very little about you. It's a lot of stage, a lot of theater, all with the aim of pleasing others and making a good impression. But that doesn't last much longer than a few months.

Human beings are full of expectations. And that's precisely where their frustrations come from. These are our feelings, generated for who knows what reason and projected onto others. First, we create the expectation and focus it on someone else; then, because the focus of the expectation hasn't come true (*strange if it did...*), resentment, frustration and disappointment follow. My invitation here is not to submit to mistaken expectations or to do this to others.

Have you ever heard the old saying: "Couples' difficulties are solved in bed"? I find this supposed truth desperately poor. For sure, the bed will be the scene where the relationship began - and where it will end.

I've heard men say that they went out at night, drank, met a girl and took her to their apartment. They had sex all night and when he woke up in the morning, without the effects of alcohol, he found her naked next to him. He felt so bad about her company that he called a cab to get her to leave as soon as possible. What a painful experience for both of them!

Let's be real and have real relationships. The best antidote to expectations is to really get to know people. And for that, one night is too little.

THE DESIRE FOR CONTROL AND ITS DAMAGES

There are two concomitant characteristics in almost all human beings. They are as common as they are paradoxical. At the same time as we find it difficult to make decisions, to define the direction of our lives, we also want to give orders of all kinds to others, to determine what the people in our relationships should do. We rarely stop to think about it. Strange as it may seem, even if you don't know what to do with yourself, you firmly believe that you have all the answers to someone else's questions - even if you haven't been asked.

It's part of our nature. We all want to be in charge, to direct, to lead. It's a constant, permanent desire. We want others to agree with us, to think the way we think. And this manifests itself in all the variables of human relationships, in very different ways.

Observe a child, who is usually very skillful, full of tricks to command their parents, to get what they want. He cries until he turns purple, refuses to eat, says he's afraid of this or that, and so he gains ground in his quest for what he wants. She creates alibis to migrate to her parents' bed in the dead of night. This isn't childish mean-spiritedness; it's human nature. How many pampering treats, how many presents, how many nights in the parents' bed, how much indulgence does a little one not gain by using their ability to control?

The child's sense of fragility and dependence on their parents, the world and their surroundings may be one of the reasons why they try to take on this role of wanting to be in charge of everything. It's as if, by magic, the situation is reversed. They now have the power, they control their parents and thus fantasize about incorporating their powers.

On the other hand, many parents look at their child as if they were incompetent and devoid of thought. They decide everything for them. They don't have the patience to sit down and talk. They give orders and are bossy.

In general, there are two scenarios: either the parents are controlling and bossy, or the children try to take on this role.

Look around you and realize how common and almost natural this scenario is in the daily lives of some families. And that's a danger! If parents don't realize early on that they are being controlled, the situation will tend to perpetuate itself. The child will use increasingly sophisticated means of control. As they grow up, they will try to repeat these mechanisms in all the other contexts they find themselves in. Therefore, a child who works like this from an early age and therefore lives with the feeling that they are powerful, will be an adult with great possibilities of creating conflicts, who will tend towards authoritarianism and will be frustrated because the world - which doesn't welcome or support them like their parents - will often contradict them.

In general, this innate controlling tendency in human beings develops imperceptibly, unconsciously. The controlling adult hardly ever goes about devising and planning ways to dominate situations. Even if his actions are objectively harmful to him and to others, there is no objective evil in his intentions. He's just acting as he's used to acting - playing games, embarrassing, harassing, demanding. These are people who use all kinds of arguments and even threats to get what they want.

So they're able to say things like that:

"I don't know if it's worth going on together... You need to change your ways!"

"If you don't do what I ask you to do, you can't count on me for anything else."

"Don't talk to me again if you don't accept what I'm asking."

Ultimately, if convincing and pressuring the other person doesn't work, it could evolve into blackmail. They're almost dictators. Relational dictators!

Of course, relationships involving controlling parties are very complicated, even unhealthy. Let's look at the other side of the coin described above: "bossy" parents. These are the types I see a lot in my practice.

It's very common to see parents who are convinced that only they know what's good for their children. These parents then subject their children to routines, activities and obligations of their choice. In this case, we have parents who decide everything for their children, who don't let them act for themselves, who make up their children's school subjects and choose their clothes and company. They don't allow teenagers to go out at night with their friends because they fear they won't know how to behave properly. The answers they give their children about their arbitrariness could be summed up in the following formula: "We know what's best for you!"

What kind of young man will he be? Probably a completely insecure person, with impaired evaluation and decision-making skills. These young people will grow up to be omissive and limited adults, who will have many difficulties with colleagues and superiors at work, spouses, friends, etc.

If before, with controlling children, we had apparently submissive parents, here the relationship is reversed. One way or another, there is nothing healthy about these relationships. A child deciding absolutely everything for themselves, with all their lack of discernment and inexperience, is just as inappropriate as a child who can't decide anything at all.

It's important to stress that, in reality, there is a complicity between the one who is in charge and the other who apparently obeys. It's a symbiosis, in a pair that works in a similar way, because both are controllers - one through activity and the other through passivity. You can see that these pairs seek each other out or attract each other. Hunger and the desire to eat come together.

Pay attention to the way some people talk to us. We're expressing our thoughts, having a conversation, telling them something that's important to us, but our interlocutor doesn't really listen to us. They're just waiting for an opportunity to talk about something else that has nothing to do with what we're talking about. In fact, they want to be heard and have no interest in actually listening to us. It's a frequent example of the desire for control that presents itself in everyday life.

In the life of a married couple, these control mechanisms thrive. The man has to ask his wife's permission to play soccer with friends after work. The woman can't go out with her friends for *happy hour* without her husband's agreement. At a children's party, they both have to go, even if one of them doesn't want to. One always chooses the movie or restaurant to go to. The way one dresses depends on the other's agreement. There's no way you won't have lunch with your husband's parents on Sundays. And there are countless other situations that you, the reader, can think of right now.

One way of observing the greater or lesser presence of these desires for control in each of us is to contemplate the degree of irritation with which we react when someone disagrees or acts differently from what we expect. We need to know that this desire to control everything is atavistic in human beings, so don't feel sick if you notice these thoughts bubbling up in your mind. The good thing would be, when we notice the presence of these control mechanisms, not to submit to them, leaving them in the background, in a "water bath". Instead of letting them control us, it's healthy not to give them space to run our lives.

A good way to combat the bossiness we carry within us is to ask someone close and intimate to help us, to alert us to any manifestations of this bossy attitude.

In any case, we should always keep an eye on our thoughts, our actions and also on the way our peers, friends, colleagues and family express themselves and act. Active observation can be an antidote to the **art of being unhappy**.

PARENTS WHO INFANTILIZE THEIR CHILDREN

Sufferings, difficulties, problems. We all know how uncomfortable and difficult life's circumstances can be. That's why we try to do everything we can to ensure that the people we love don't experience difficulties. This is particularly true of the relationship between parents and children. However, there is a great risk in this: the risk of infantilizing children.

Perhaps you yourself have done this or have seen someone meddling too much in your children's lives. Whether it's because they want to show you the best way, teach you, pass on experiences, or because they want to avoid suffering. For example, the child doesn't do his or her schoolwork, or does badly at school, and then there are the adults doing homework, calculating, cutting out, pasting, in short, doing schoolwork so that the child gets better grades. The child doesn't do an agreed-upon chore around the house, such as washing the dishes; immediately, one of the parents does the dishes, instead of talking to the child about their "forgetfulness". The common explanation given by parents for doing it instead of talking and confronting their children is this: "I did it so it wouldn't bother me." Certainly, the annoyance avoided in childhood will come back much more strongly in later life.

Why do parents tend to act like this? I can think of a few answers: "We want them to learn"; "We know what to do to make them do well"; "To reduce their nervousness"; "I suffered in childhood and I don't want my child to go through that too" etc.

Imagine a child who has difficulties relating to his peers at school. He comes home crying because his classmates don't pay attention to him and don't invite him to play. Instead of sitting down with the child, listening to them, presenting them with alternatives and trying to let them learn how to get along in practice, some parents are capable of calling the parents of other children to get them to change their attitude towards their child.

Another possibility: the child has trouble sleeping in their own bed and goes to their parents' bed at night. The parents tend to acquiesce. As a result, the couple's bed becomes the family bed for a long time. To make life easier for the couple, the tendency is to let the child sleep together. The healthiest thing would be to have a chat with the little one, take them back to their room, leave a lamp on, spend some time reading, sitting in an armchair. Generally, children with these nocturnal fears give in to their parents' firm and enlightening stance.

Notice in these two examples the subtlety of the desire for control that little ones have over their parents. Children are mischievous, clever, intelligent and cunning *little beings*. They act in a precise, focused, unconscious and unprejudiced way. In any case, they try to take over their parents' space and power. They set up little traps in family life. It's up to the parents, with subtlety, affection and respect, to dismantle them - not least because then they can help their child not to carry these vices through life.

It's all very ingenious, with the risk of disrupting the formation of children's personalities. It is clear that, with the condescension of adults, children soon lose their sense of limits, as they realize, intuitively, that they have an enormous capacity to manipulate their parents, to get anything they want. Young people often fail to develop their emotional and cognitive skills as a result of this inadequate support from their parents. As they grow up, these individuals show signs of infantilization, with inordinate dependence. In adolescence and adulthood, they use these prerogatives unconsciously, manipulating their parents and demanding material, emotional and financial support beyond the limits of a healthy and possible relationship.

These adult children perceive themselves as fragile, insecure and lacking the initiative to take charge of their lives. They constantly need and appeal to their parents. Consciously and objectively, they look to their parents for a direct solution to their daily problems. They need them to pay their bills, they constantly ask for money, to take their grandchild to and from school, to have the cleaning lady clean their apartment.

Look at the unconscious way in which they ask for help through the messes and nonsense in their lives. Then, the child who used to play with tears and antics turns into an adult who has to go to his parents to pick him up from a traffic stop because he hasn't paid his MOT; who needs help because the electricity has been cut off at home because he forgot to pay the bill; who is overdrawn and can't pay it off, etc. Of course, in these situations, the parents who infantilized their children rush to cover for them. And the unhealthy cycle is reinvigorated.

To the parents who identify with this text, I say don't blame yourself, but rethink the relationship. Take care not to enter into a process of self-pity, of justification - "I did it because I love my child". Nor cultivate the crucial question that may cross your mind: "Where did we go wrong?"

Now, raising children is not a mathematical game of trial and error. It's a dynamic process, which changes with our experiences, with the passage of time, and which will also depend on each child's way of being. Avoid self-punishment, because it's not about getting it right or wrong, but about evaluating what you can do differently, with the aim of changing your attitude.

It's important for parents to realize that children have to find their own alternatives and choose their own paths. They need to experience frustrations, face losses, in short, realize that they are capable of taking charge of their own lives. Some simple but healthy attitudes help children to feel competent: allowing them to take a bath when they ask; letting them try to clean themselves after urinating or defecating; ordering them to put away the toys they have used; letting them eat alone, even if they dirty the floor; not caring if they get dirty in the square... Of course, all this with parental supervision.

The difficulties are visible from an early age, but it is in adolescence that they take on their most dramatic form. Infantilized youngsters tend to vary between a, shall we say, lazy lukewarmness and disproportionate aggression, especially when they are contradicted or their whims are not met. These teenagers can have serious relationship and learning difficulties and end up getting involved in a variety of problems, some of them more serious. They often end up with teenage pregnancies, alcohol or drug use, poor school performance and aggression.

* * *

I have a hypothesis about enlightened girls who get pregnant in their teens. I realize that the pregnancy was not due to a lack of knowledge. The point is that getting pregnant could be an unconscious alibi, like a safe-conduct for the young woman to remain in her parents' home. With the pregnancy will come a baby who needs to be taken care of, and that's where the mother comes in, who will also continue to be protected. That way, she won't have to face the challenges that life throws at her. Note that, in general, these young women get pregnant by completely infantilized boys, who won't be able or willing to take on fatherhood.

Another idea I have is about some young people who use marijuana or drink too much, to the point where they can't manage their school, professional and relationship lives. It's a perfect, unconscious psychological strategy to avoid committing to their lives. Parents are left paying the bills, trying to find jobs or getting them out of all sorts of trouble, even the police. In this case, using alcohol (or marijuana) can become a protective shield against the demands of adult life. And the greatest danger is that parents feel guilty for their children's bad habits, so they don't allow themselves to change their attitude towards this unhealthy symbiosis that has been created.

* * *

I'd like to present another angle on the issue of infantilization. I've seen some parents cultivating the seed of eternal dependence in one of their children, so that they always have them by their side. Without realizing it, the parents end up choosing one of their children so that they will always be close by. They then spend their lives, without realizing it, negotiating so that this offspring doesn't become independent and abandon them.

It's as if they're saying: "This one will stay here to look after us." With this child they will be more than permissive. Even if they don't like it, they won't take too kindly to repeated drinking bouts, drug addiction and other destructive behavior. They'll also shower the youngster with gifts and perks - money for parties and shopping, a car here, an apartment there...

Initially - and for a long time - this son will like and encourage this relationship of interests, but over time he will realize that his life has been boycotted. It won't be long before he realizes that life has passed him by, but he has remained stagnant, relying on the kindness of his parents. Again, the result will be a frustrated and compromised individual in his development, mixing his actions between passivity and aggression. These young people tend to be angry, because they don't fully understand what has prevented them from progressing in life, but they sense that their relationship with their parents has not been well managed.

* * *

In all the cases mentioned here, it is advisable to give children and young people space and let them live their lives. This doesn't mean abandoning them to their fate. What is appropriate is to let them get things right and wrong according to the circumstances and situations. Always talk about what went right and what went wrong, but without playing the role of know-it-all.

Another warning to parents. Look at how you feel about your children. For some, being a father is not a pleasant experience at all. They feel overwhelmed and even discontented by the natural demands of parenthood. These feelings can make fathers want to get rid of the demands of caring for their children as soon as possible. They look at their pubescent or adolescent children and imagine them ready to face life. So they encourage them to go out at night, drink and not have to tell anyone about what they do or where they go.

To fathers who don't feel much affection or pleasure in fatherhood, I suggest that you don't beat yourself up, don't blame yourself; just accept the situation. If, at some point, you are asked for more affection, cuddling and swearing of love, reveal these limitations to your children. Talking about our difficulties usually brings greater intimacy and closeness.

I'll end with my mother's maxim about dealing with children: "When in doubt, tighten - don't loosen."

BRAVERY IN THE FACE OF FRUSTRATED EXPECTATIONS

If there's one thing in my life that I observe incessantly and tirelessly, it's my possible irritation, my annoyance at experiences that frustrate me. I never neglect my irascible potential. This is not some psychiatrist's unreasonable mania. In the past, I've been a more angry, irritable person. Today, however, I believe I have a satisfactory handle on my tendencies at the cost of a lot of attention and discipline. I always keep an eye on my anger and, when I realize that it can grow, even in situations where I'm *quite right,* I quickly try to manage it. I've done well.

I'm not advocating **zero irritation**, that would be impossible. But I realize that when I'm angry and irascible, my mind becomes unhealthy; I'm overweight, which I don't like and doesn't do me any good. I take care of myself not because of any philosophical or religious doctrine, but to take care of my mental health and those around me. When we're angry, any look or word from those around us can generate a crisis, a conflict. Anger takes away our ability to think. We are left at the mercy of our impulses, which is very dangerous.

Irritation is atavistic; it's part of human nature. The human being is not a nice, gentle animal, willing to do anything. Even before it acquires verbal language, when it communicates only with moans and cries, it already makes clear its innate tendency to get angry. It grows up a little more and starts physically attacking anyone it dislikes.

Some more, some less, we have good and bad inclinations in our being - and certainly irritation, violence and impatience are some of the characteristics inscribed in our DNA.

So let's talk about everyday life, about situations that can affect all of us. **Why, after all, do we get angry and irritated when faced with trivial**

difficulties? In this text, I'm going to mention various sources of anger. I'll start with our **expectations**. Abusive reactions are usually responses to frustrations which, in turn, stem from the expectations we have, the search for results or things we long for but which have not come true. If a girl expects her boyfriend to give her flowers for her birthday, but he gives her perfume, this could be a reason for her to dislike the gift and get angry with her lover. Expectations dashed! You see, the trigger for annoyance is not in the gift or the boyfriend, but in the girlfriend's imagination.

It's clear that our unconscious is impregnated with repressed feelings that are not perceptible in our conscious. Therefore, one event can trigger disproportionate reactions. If we've experienced mistreatment or abuse in childhood, any experience reminiscent of that experience will make us very angry. It's as if the current event opens a repressed floodgate of annoyances from the past. A flood of angry feelings emerges.

When we don't get or receive what we want, we lose patience very easily. We want our opinions to be accepted; we want everyone to agree with our ideas; we expect our plans to turn out the way we planned them. If thwarted, we can lose our temper.

Reality shows us all the time that our expectations are often frustrated. If I get angry about this, I have two options. Change the world or change my mind. In other words, I alone am responsible for my angry reactions. It's good that it's my responsibility, because I can be the agent of change. Notice that I didn't use the word "blame", but "responsibility". "Blame" is usually accompanied by an impulse to punish - in other words, unconsciously some may repeat the cycle: they argue, get angry, fight, feel guilty and find a way to punish themselves. This creates a repetitive and endless cycle. If I feel responsible for the wrongdoing, I will confront it - and with the determination not to repeat it.

There is another unconscious mechanism that can explain our bravery: **the desire for control**. It stimulates our imagination to think and act as if we could take control of everything and everyone. As if we were the "powerful boss", a character from Italian mafia movies.

I remember a lady who had just entered the menopause. There was a drop in her hormone levels and in her sex drive. To make matters worse, gynecologists now didn't recommend hormone replacement. Her partner was irritated by her lack of sexual desire, as if she were neglecting him. He wanted to have sex anyway, because it was a demonstration that he was loved. The desire for control is disguised as the desire to be loved.

The presence of the desire for control creates a false idea that we are very important, that the world should bow down to our wishes. The more important we think we are, the greater the disappointments and irritations. Conflicts are imminent in the face of a controller: either you submit and get angry quietly, or you explode and send them away. A good remedy in these times when we think we're special is to follow what teenagers say in their slang: "Less, less..." I would say:

"Much less! We don't have all this ball."

Traffic is a good setting for observing how we react. We are easily irritated by the attitudes of other drivers. Sometimes we're right; sometimes we're not, because we often have the same attitudes as those who have annoyed us, committing the same mistakes that others make and which make us angry.

It's the same with everything else in life: when we're late for an appointment, we expect understanding from those who are waiting for us; when we're the ones waiting, we demand explanations and apologies from those who are late.

In order to better understand our anger, it's interesting to look at another mechanism present in our imagination, called **projection**. Through it, we try to put the feelings that bother us onto others. It would be something like this: the bank teller isn't in a good mood with me, but in fact I'm the one who's annoyed because I think he took too long to serve me. If I'm suspicious, I think others are against me, but in fact I'm the one who created this foolish idea and I project it onto others. This attempt to get rid of our anxieties by projecting them onto others doesn't work, because they remain intense inside our heads. It's like a boomerang that we throw far away, but then it comes back to us.

If we can perceive this movement that makes us angry, that's a good start. If we are the source of the problem, we can also be the solution, which is very interesting. In this context, it's a good idea to undertake some re-education, to pay close attention to our reactions, trying to absorb and realize that our irritability won't open any doors.

Sometimes banal everyday situations can be experienced by some as provocative. Examples: an argument about politics; an accidental bump in the street; different opinions about soccer; a disagreement of some kind; hearing someone say a bad word to you...

I remember a friend who was upset when he was called "cuckold", a word that suggested he had been betrayed by his wife. In general, it's something that intensely hurts men's feelings. However, at the time, this friend was single (!!!!!) and had no recollection of having experienced betrayal in the past. In other words, he couldn't possibly be a "cuckold". But, insanely, he couldn't think for a second and realized that the apparent offense only made sense because in his imagination he gave it an almost real meaning.

This case shows that the anger is not even connected to the event itself, but to the representativeness of the word in our emotional memory. For example, if we have been mistreated and disqualified by our parents, by a partner, by the boss, in short, our memory is impregnated with a feeling of worthlessness. Any word that sounds like disqualification will unleash past and pent-up anger that mixes with the current event and can become an explosive tsunami.

* * *

It's important to emphasize that in my reflections on the bravery of everyday life, I exclude people with psychiatric illnesses, such as those with bipolar mood disorder, anxiety disorders (obsessive-compulsive, phobias, panic syndrome), depression and drug addiction, among others. Many people with irritable outbursts may have a psychiatric illness. It's likely that, with the use of some medication, your anger will subside.

* * *

Of course, in order to deal better with anger, you don't have to become an apathetic, indifferent and passive person, incapable of reacting. One tip I give when faced with heated arguments and a high level of irritation is to postpone the discussion until another time. We will always have the opportunity, on another day, to return to the subject with someone who has treated us in a way we don't think is appropriate.

Let's never forget that **expectation is the mother of frustration**. Oh, and the use of alcohol greatly increases our aggressive potential.

THE LACK OF INTIMACY BETWEEN COUPLES

When couples get married, they promise: "*Till death do us part*". However, they don't count on problems of communication, of everyday life.

Communication can be verbal and non-verbal. Verbally, we can express our thoughts and feelings through speech. Non-verbally, through gestures, facial expressions, noises and even silence. Newborn babies, for example, can only communicate by crying.

The responsibility for problems relating to relationships basically lies with each one of us, even if the other person has been inappropriate in putting forward their point of view. And that's why we're here, analyzing ourselves and trying to improve our relationship with life.

One of the contexts in which communication difficulties occur most intensely and constantly is in couples' relationships. It's not uncommon for us to express ourselves in an intemperate way. When we talk to our partner, we sometimes do so in an irritable, excessive and even invasive way. This approach generates discomfort and an automatic refusal to move towards a resolution. Thus, the problems remain and even take on greater proportions.

Another important point in communication refers to who listens and returns the information received, demonstrating that the message has been understood. However clear the message may be, there is the possibility that the receiver will understand it the way they want to. On the one hand, there's the speaker; on the other, there's the listener who re-reads what they've heard. It sounds crazy, but yes, communication can be clear, the sender may have spoken with delicacy and respect and yet the other person may not agree.

I'll illustrate with a conversation I witnessed with a couple. They had a dog with dermatitis, for which they had tried various treatments without success. The husband said that perhaps they should think about leaving her out in the sun for longer. The wife was indignant and said that she already spent a lot of time with the animal and that she wouldn't be able to do her own thing. She raised her voice. The husband replied:

- I didn't ask you to take her out in the sun, I'm not asking you to perform better with the dog. I can do it myself.

In fact, I didn't notice any demands or irritation on the husband's part, but even so, the woman, in her imagination, thought she was being demanded. Perhaps she was demanded and charged a lot in her childhood and carries this ghost in her unconscious. Fortunately, the conversation evolved fruitfully. But you can see how we are impregnated with rancor and how easy it is for our unconscious to distort the meaning of what has been said, of what we have heard.

Reinforcing this concept: successful communication depends not only on who speaks, but also on who listens. In addition to the spoken word, there are our thoughts and moods, which are part of this process and influence it. Of course, it's hard for people to realize how much they interfere, for better or worse, in the exercise of communication.

A thought disorder can make people more suspicious. They are more likely to feel accused by others - either by their words or by the tone of their voice. Mood is also responsible for distortions in communication. Imagine a sad person, dejected by the defeat of their soccer team; at that moment, a word can be distorted in their imagination, due to their dejected, irritated mood.

* * *

In order to deal better with communication, I've come up with a few recommendations that would suit anyone, but are perfectly suited to relationships between couples.

The moment. It's important to choose the right time to speak. Popular wisdom is really wise when it says: "Dirty laundry is washed at home." Intimate conversations should really be intimate, without children or other people around. You should also take care to understand your spouse's receptiveness and mood to talk about the subject at that moment. Ah, important: it's always a bad idea to talk to someone who has been drinking, even if they're not actually intoxicated. This also applies to those who have used other drugs or are under the influence of tranquilizers.

The content. Analyze the subject well. Look at the issue you want to deal with. Make sure you don't mix up the issues, so as not to confuse the situation. Good content is made up of *well-placed words*, with objectivity and truth. No rumors, no gossip, no illusions.

The form. Finally, breathe calmly and adjust your tone of voice and manner of speaking. It's no good just choosing the right moment to address a necessary issue. It's essential to take care of *how* you speak. Think about it. How many arguments between you and your partner have ended up being about a harsh word that was said or a shout that was given? Shouting, boisterousness, demands and threats are all harmful to a successful conversation.

* * *

You've arranged to pick up your girlfriend at home at 7 p.m. to go to the movies. Afterwards, you planned to have dinner and go out dancing. The movie starts at 8pm. At the appointed time, you are in front of her house, as agreed. She's often late. You get annoyed. She gets in her car at 7:20. There's still time to get to the cinema and catch the movie. But you're uncomfortable and feel disrespected. You then have several options:

He naturally expresses his annoyance at the delay.

He gets angry and doesn't want to go to the movies.

Get over it, even if you're upset, and get on with your schedule.

He cares about what happened, but leaves it until after the movie.

Of course, it's always best to offer the other person what we're feeling, but we *have to be very careful when we speak,* when we express what we're feeling, to avoid *being* rude and making the situation even worse. There is no ready-made recipe. Everything will depend more on how your boyfriend interprets it than on the fact itself. In this case, the emotional, the imaginary, will weigh more heavily than reality. Of course, the girlfriend's response is very important, as it can calm or increase her partner's discomfort.

* * *

Another complicating factor in marital relationships is demanding, the **desire for control**. I think it's fatal when one spouse wants to be in charge of the other's life. "You're not going to play soccer with your friends today, I don't want to be alone at home"; "My wife doesn't go out in that skirt, it attracts too much attention!"; "I'll pay for it, so I'll choose the restaurant"; "I don't want you to visit your mother".

I'll illustrate with the story of a friend who was unhappy and annoyed with his wife who had lost the desire to have sex. She was going through the menopause and evidently, for hormonal reasons, she had lost her libido and vaginal lubrication, making it difficult to have sex. But I realized that he was denying this reality and was feeling despised. Of course, this person had a feeling of low self-esteem in his emotional core, which led him to deny reality. Not least because the wife herself was also upset by the loss of libido. Nature, from the point of view of sexuality, is crueler with women, because men still have desire.

Sex life can be wonderful, but it can also be the source of a lot of marital tension and annoyance. I say this because some couples put the success or failure of their relationship down to sex. I notice that some women have sex without feeling any real pleasure, because their partners are more concerned with their own pleasure and forget to look at their partner's reaction. Other times, men have premature ejaculation, which makes it impossible for the woman to have a pleasurable sex life. Men tend to deny the harm and pretend that everything is fine. I've heard from women who, when told about it, their partner replied that he had never had this problem, suggesting that the problem arose in this new relationship.

The root of this is the need that some people have to control situations. Nothing can go against their expectations, including the steps of the person with whom they should be sharing life with affinity and complicity. I've already heard from a girl who got angry and felt disqualified when her husband wore a different outfit to the one she had chosen for him to wear to work.

I'm allowed to make a prediction about the best partnership model for a couple. I think that for a relationship to have fewer conflicts, it is essential that the parties maintain their individuality. Each person should maintain their own tastes and customs, taking care of themselves and then the couple.

THE ART OF SABOTAGING YOUR OWN COMPANY

One subject that has been relegated to oblivion, despite its recurrence and importance, is professional relationships. It is striking how little importance we give to emotional life in professional performance. There seems to be a dichotomy in which only the professional's intelligence and preparation to achieve their goals are of interest.

The priority is production; the focus is on results. And there's no mistake about that. However, attention needs to be paid to something indispensable, which is the employee's emotional state. It would be very opportune and healthy in a work context if coexistence favored more truthful and transparent relationships. This would certainly lead to a better quality of life and also greater productivity, efficiency and complicity among those involved in the tasks.

There's no mistake in focusing on results, because that's why human beings come together in work organizations, to produce. But there's no reason not to pay attention to people's needs.

We don't have a culture of finding out if colleagues or subordinates have something to say, or if there's something bothering them, if they're hurt or don't like something that's been said. We live focused on appearances, on what seems appropriate to say, leaving aside the truth in relationships of any kind.

In some of the consultancy work I've done for companies and institutions, I've come across bosses with a bossy profile and absolutist attitudes. When I say *bossy*, I don't mean that they are bad people or that they want to harm and mistreat the employee. However, they are managers who only pay attention to what they think and to their own content and concepts; the others who work around them are just depositories of their ideas. They have no interest in listening to the opinions of those lower down the hierarchy.

Their employees have to produce exactly the way they think is right, without negotiation. The aggravating aspect of this way of working is that these managers are completely unaware of it.

This type of behavior is harmful and detrimental to good professional relations. Employees subjected to such environments tend to become silent and avoid resolving and cooperative attitudes. The result is clearly visible in the company's productivity. And here's a beautiful paradox. The arrogant and overly demanding boss believes that he will get the most out of his employees with his method, but it is precisely this way of acting that hinders the development of everyone in the company, also preventing a good environment for employees and resulting in financial results that fall short of possibilities and expectations.

In fact, we are already in the habit of withholding the truth. We are addicted to excessively polished behavior, made up of appearances. At work, where we need to fit in or else we won't be accepted, this tendency is naturally accentuated. Add to this a castrating boss and the result is an environment of extreme artificiality. This is bad for the person, as it interferes with their mood and their conscience, but it is also "toxic" for others and for the organization.

What kind of relationship are we developing if we can't be truthful and honest? That's why I always encourage truthfulness and openness, both for employees and employers. Of course, you have to be careful not to hurt feelings or jeopardize something you can't give up. But little by little, with dialog, patience and good intentions, it is possible to get out of the spiral of silence and pretense that we tend to get ourselves into. The key word is to **express yourself**.

Nowadays, the difference between a boss and a leader is a very common, repetitive and tiresome subject. In fact, what distinguishes one from the other is not the degree of technical knowledge for the task, but the personality traits. The boss is the guy who wants to be in charge, to command, to show that he knows everything and decides everything. He is powerful, grandiose, omnipotent. He wants profits and the company to grow, but he despises his employees and has no eyes or ears for them. Of course, behind this behavior hides a fragile and insecure human being.

The true manager, the leader, is not arrogant, megalomaniacal or omnipotent. He brings people close to him, asks for their opinions, discusses projects and plans. He doesn't shy away from showing doubts, changing his mind or his path. He doesn't take offense at employees who disagree or think differently from him. He encourages them to say what they think. Of course, this attitude doesn't mean submission or weakness on the part of those who command and guide. What we have here is a self-assured, respectful man who doesn't need to step on others to grow and show his competence. The true authority that a manager enjoys is earned, it is built.

For those in charge, I recommend talking openly with their bosses, making honest comments and asking them to do the same. As for employees, I advise them to have an open attitude towards their peers, creating an environment in which the truth can circulate, and to gradually, as far as possible, establish this relationship with their superiors.

And that goes for our personal relationships too, of course. I myself feel very satisfied and secure when a patient tells me the truth about something that is bothering them in their treatment, in our conversations. I don't want stratified relationships in my work, where I'm the powerful doctor and the other person is the passive, sickly patient. I also really like it when a child is allowed to think or act differently from me. Of course, applause and praise are great, they do us good. We should always offer people that. But not just that.

In the past, we lived through a period of discipline, in which people followed rules, did tasks and kept to schedules. Today we have a performance society, in which everyone needs to perform more and more, which effectively distances people. In the corporate world, the Americans coined the expressions "*loosers*", for losers, and "*winners*", for *winners*. It's no coincidence that in environments where what matters least is the person, the incidence of depression, panic disorder, alcohol and drug addiction has increased.

I think that the next few decades will see a greater understanding, investment and development of the workings of the human mind. Currently, when hiring a professional, the most important factors are their knowledge and their CV. However, as time goes by, the eyes of human resources personnel will tend to turn to the person's behavior at work. It's already a saying in the industry: "Knowledge hires, behavior fires."

Between the rules of the past and the pressures of the present, we must seek balance and, in people management, know how to speak and listen, manage and lead. It is with this view of emotional management that I am sometimes invited into the intimacy of some institutions. I notice a certain fear on the part of managers when I arrive to take part in work meetings. It seems as if I'm going to point the finger at inappropriate behavior. At the end of these consultancies, I notice satisfaction and gratitude about my interventions. It's not that I'm a magician or anything; the point is that all organizations, as places where people relate to each other, may need guidance and clarification in order for things to flow better.

A GOOD WORD IS NOT ENOUGH!

I'm very fond of sayings, platitudes and aphorisms. They are popular, empirical perceptions, based on easily verifiable realities and stabilized in centuries-old expressions. In fact, in general, the sayings correspond to the facts. However, if there's one I don't agree with, it's this: "For a good understanding, half a word is enough." No! No! The right thing to say would be: "For a good understanding, half a word is **not** enough!"

Verbal language is unique to human beings. And we've developed it so much and reached such levels of refinement that the words combined don't always refer directly to the objects to which they refer. I'm talking about figures of speech, which are subjective ways of saying things. We use and abuse metaphors, hyperbole, metonyms and the like.

We also speak in indirect ways. Instead of clearly saying, "I'm against that," we say, "That doesn't sound like a good idea..." We hide behind plurals or abstract entities to take responsibility for what we say and, sometimes, to play the good guy. Then, instead of: "I've decided to fire you", the boss says: "I think you've exhausted your ability to cooperate with the company and we've decided to relieve you of your duties..."

In short, we make excessive use of the many linguistic resources available to us. We abuse speech and writing tools that are really useful and we often end up hindering rather than facilitating communication. By mistakenly using these tools, which should serve to improve understanding, we are not clear, we don't offer the other person what we are thinking. And we create conflicts or totally inappropriate expectations.

Here's a very common example, a situation we come across every day. You meet a close friend or family member who doesn't quite understand you and automatically asks: "Are you all right?" No, everything is not fine. You know that. But the tendency, more often than not, is to swallow the truth and say: "Everything's fine."

Think about it: how many times have you answered this common question truthfully? In fact, from being so common at the start of conversations, this question, which used to be "Are you okay?", has become "Are you okay?" - and is now reduced to a simple, hurried "Everything?". I realize that this type of interaction works more like a ritual than a real communication between mutually interested people. Sometimes, we even hope that the person we're asking - "Everything OK?" - doesn't really answer and prefers the protocol, unthinking answer - "Yes, everything", even if they're not.

One way or another, what's missing is the **whole**, complete **word**. It's about saying what's really going on, what we want, what we don't want, in short. Half a word is not enough. Half words - hidden feelings, uncommunicated interests, exaggerated grievances, oblique expressions... All this only makes relationships more difficult. Half words are also communicated through sour faces, grimaces, tantrums, bad moods, etc.

Let's be direct!

I once invited myself to sit at the table of two friends who were already having lunch. After I'd finished my lunch, one of the friends asked if I could leave them alone, as they had something private to talk about. At first, I was surprised by the request. However, I applauded the guy's attitude, as he really acted like a big man. Why? Because he was being honest and very clear with me and his interests. He didn't mince words. And I didn't take offense; on the contrary, I complimented him on his clarity and elegance in setting out what was best for him at the time. Imagine if he hadn't spoken and I had remained seated, the probable annoyance I would have unknowingly caused two friends.

I also remember a message I left for my bank manager. Days passed without her getting back to me. When I spoke to her about the message, she told me that she had tried to call me, but couldn't find me. This was obviously a lame excuse. I was truthful and said that I didn't like this solution and that, if she left me a message, I would make many attempts to find her. Of course, I always spoke very gently, but without losing my objectivity.

Another half-word story. I often make coffee in my office and whenever I do, I offer it to my patients. On one occasion, a patient entered the room and smelled the coffee made in a previous session. He said: "That smells good!" I noticed his half-words and kept quiet. He changed the subject and went on with another conversation. After a while, I returned to the coffee and asked him why he had remarked on the smell. He embarrassedly admitted that he'd like a coffee. I made the drink and took the opportunity to talk about the risks of not getting what you want when you hide behind incomplete communications.

One more. A single friend took an interest in a girl and asked her out to dinner. She was a little frightened by his boldness and asked: "Are you having second thoughts?" He had presence of mind and said that, more than that, he had second, third and fourth intentions. He didn't mince his words, and the relationship between the two evolved, apparently with fifth intentions! Imagine if he had replied that he had no second thoughts? You'd both lose.

An inexhaustible source of cases to illustrate the harm of half-words is the marital relationship. For example, in sexual matters. The sexual relationship is damaged and unpleasant when the man has premature ejaculation. The only way to solve this problem is for the partner to speak clearly about the difficulty. Men tend to deny their impotence and pretend that everything is fine with their sexual performance. If the partner doesn't express her dissatisfaction in words, there is a possibility that she will pull away as a result of somatization, such as vaginal pain during intercourse, frigidity or loss of libido. In this case, it's the body that does the talking.

But why do we tend to use half-words? One clue to solving this riddle lies in childhood. Children see their parents as special beings, endowed with superpowers, to the point of finding out what they think and want. It creates a lot of anxiety in children's imaginations to realize the degree of dependence on their parents and, as a result, the possibility of being abandoned.

To combat these terrible fantasies, they want to be like their parents, powerful and controlling. In this way, they use tricks to achieve their goals and obtain benefits. So they cry, get upset, don't want to eat, feel afraid, say it hurts here and there, etc. All of this is normal, but it is indicative of grandiose, almost delusional thinking stemming from a child's imaginary world. We call this type of thinking magical. Children imagine that everything they think and want can come true, even if they don't fully say what they want. They get used to using half-words, either verbally or in their attitudes. I'm talking here about children who already know and could express themselves in words, of course.

Of course, all children tend to use these mechanisms, but not all of them will make it to adulthood, so to speak. It's up to parents to watch out for this childish game of trying to take advantage and control the environment. The best course of action is to sit down with your children, talk, explain and not submit to their control. Of course, always with affection, care and attention, but firmly. No threats or violence!

The problem of half-words is serious when it happens to adults. It's all very well for children to use these mechanisms of thinking that they will be understood by using magical tricks, but in the adult world this is chaotic.

We often hear things like: "I hinted at it with my attitude"; "I turned my back on him"; "I showed my anger"; "I disagreed by keeping quiet"; "I left it between the lines"; "I sent the message via my colleague"; "I withdrew from the room"; "I didn't want to have sex anymore". These oblique ways of trying to be understood are still childish, like thinking we're so important that others have to figure out what we want, even if we don't use clear verbal language.

We certainly won't be fully understood with half-words, because the other person will complete the understanding in the way that is best for them. We often hear this: *"I didn't say anything because I didn't know what his reaction would be..."* Be patient! How can we know the other person's reaction to something we've offered through words or actions? There's no way of knowing - and what's more, once we've spoken, it's no longer our problem, it's the other person's problem.

Why is it difficult to tell someone that we don't agree or don't like something they've said or done? Why do we want to be liked and not cause disappointment to those we're living with? But for us to be truly admired and understood, there is only one way: the truth. And it's only built with complete words.

LOVE AND SEX

Marital relationships begin, remain and end for conscious or unconscious reasons. But if we want to make any distinction between types of bonds, the clearest differentiation there is between relationships based exclusively on sex and relationships centered on admiration, attention, affection and love.

A relationship based on sex is much simpler, it starts off in a more uncomplicated way. However, its duration tends to be short and the end almost predictable. Using a figure of speech with fire (so associated with passion), this type of relationship is a fire that starts out strong, intense, but is soon extinguished. Something like a "straw fire".

A relationship based on other attributes that generate a bond may take longer to get off the ground, but tends to last longer. It's a fire that ignites little by little, but spreads and tends to last longer. Look at the sexual relationship exercised through payment. It tends to work well for those who want to satisfy their desires without any effort at conquest.

The connection that takes place through sex is almost objective, direct; sometimes it doesn't even require an exchange of words. There is an exchange of glances, instant empathy, an outpouring of desire and, finally, closeness. All the identifications that lead to this type of relationship are linked to natural and, let's say, material characteristics of people - the smell, the touch, the fluids, the voice, the body.

Among teenagers there is a mechanism called "hooking up". The "hookups" get close and, without much conversation, start exchanging kisses and hugs. This is usually all it takes, and the ritual can be repeated with other partners at the same party. Building a loving partnership, on the other hand, requires abstraction, the ability to see beyond what the eyes can see.

Sexual rapture depends on the moment, on what you see and touch at the time. It doesn't require inner elaboration. It's more hormonal, impulsive.

It's pure horniness. The bond of love, on the other hand, depends on what you feel intimately. It arises more from the inside out, in the way that each person constructs the other in their imagination, how the other fits into the desires for partnership and coexistence of those who want to conquer them. It doesn't require urgency to consummate the carnal union.

That's why I said above that a relationship based on sex tends to have a traumatic ending, in the sense that it ends abruptly, without much delay or explanation. This happens for a very simple reason: the desire that brought the parties together depends on the characteristics and conditions of the one who desires and the one who is desired. Our desires and preferences change a lot - and this influences the one who desires in the sense of making them desire something (someone) different. When the partnership is predominantly about sex, even in intense sexual relationships full of emotions and pleasures, there is the possibility of creating an existential void after the climax, the orgasm. Something like the emptiness that a drug addict feels when the hangover hits, the next day after using the drug.

A love relationship, however, can be a safer route - if you're looking for a more intimate companionship, a more lasting union. However, it is also much more complex and laborious, carries a high burden of responsibility and can scare off many people who don't think they are willing to spend all that energy on a relationship. In fact, there are those who simply don't have the capacity to live this type of relationship and so jump from sexual affair to sexual affair.

In fact, it's not so simple to fill the time you spend together in a relationship with harmony. Sex really is a good occupation. But if all you have is sex, what's left for your free time? This, among other reasons, is why romantic relationships are more difficult. It requires more commitment, more dedication, complicity, partnership and intimacy. This is the only way to spend quality time together.

It may seem silly to some, but what I realize is that it's not that uncommon for couples to simply not know what to do with each other's company. Cell phones have filled the void between couples who lack communication and complicity. They're together, but each one of them is on WhatsApp, Instagram and Facebook, not with their partner. A pleasant routine for two is a real achievement. But only this can guarantee a degree of harmony.

How *wonderful* is this popular saying: "A couple's problems are solved in bed." Now, if that were true, it would reinforce the idea that complicity in thoughts, words and reflections is not necessary to stabilize and bring a relationship to fruition. When this happens, when a couple needs to have sex to get along, the relationship's days are probably numbered.

You see, of course a satisfying sex life is good and necessary for any couple; my point is that it shouldn't be the only convergence of those in a relationship. If this is the case, it will be difficult for the relationship to break through the barrier of the ephemeral, the empty and the transitory.

I'd like to offer this reflection on relationships based on sex. Alcohol (or other drugs) is usually the great facilitator of these relationships. Barriers, fears and shyness fall away in the blink of an eye when intoxicating substances come into play. I hear sad stories from people who have spent a night with someone and, when they wake up, no longer under the influence of the drugs they've consumed, they think: "What am I doing here with this person?"; "How can I get rid of her as quickly as possible?"; "Sometimes I can't even remember her name". Sad. Very sad!

* * *

I conclude by saying that there is a natural difference in the way men and women relate to each other. Women have a more developed ability to get emotionally involved; they want more stability and know how to work for it - but they also end up being very demanding. Men, on the other hand, are generally more impulsive, intemperate and more easily *thrown* into sexual relationships. Realizing this, many women end up giving themselves away and using their bodies and their sexual possibilities as bait, as a way of attracting and obtaining male attention. Of course, they will attract men with this more impoverished profile.

I'm not trying to create guidelines or give you a manual on the best and healthiest way to have a relationship. I assume that everyone offers what they can in a relationship. There are those who are loath to be alone, who are genuinely afraid of not being together, of mating, of marriage - and so they run the risk of getting closer and seeking more and more of what they fear: being alone. Why? As a result of this phobic anxiety about not having someone, they mindlessly throw themselves into the hands or onto the lap of the first person they come across. Generally, this partnership is marked by an exaggerated need for the other person, with exaggerated expectations: "Let's see each other every day!"; "Why haven't you answered WhatsApp and my *emails*?"; "Are you going out with your friends and not me?". The other becomes the source of meaning in life, the source of energy, the source of everything.

Maintaining a loving relationship is an arduous and demanding task. It's not for amateurs. A *fit and toned body* may be a good attraction, but it will have limited reach, because there will be other *bodies* just ahead. Of course, having good sex is a stimulus to the strength of the bond, but even when there may be sexual difficulties, the couple will manage.

In order for love relationships to be more consistent and pleasurable, it is essential that there is the ingredient of individuality in the relationship. The will and desire of the individual must prevail over the social ritual that demands their conduct.

DEPRESSION, THE DISEASE OF THE CENTURY

Depression is a recurring and relevant illness in our society. We are becoming more and more depressed. Medical research suggests that 15% of the population will experience at least one depressive crisis in their lifetime. The World Health Organization reports that by 2025, depression will be the second most common illness, behind cardiovascular disease. Women are three times more depressed than men.

While its occurrence is growing, its diagnosis remains complicated. To diagnose mental illnesses such as depression, the traditional tests ordered by doctors (blood tests, CT scans, brain MRIs, electroencephalograms, etc.) are not effective. Emotional and mental disorders don't show up on tests. There is therefore a huge dependence on the psychiatrist's training, experience, preparation, sensitivity and perception in order to reach a proper diagnosis. The interview with the patient and their family is the tool used to make the diagnosis.

Psychiatrists and psychologists notice the presence of hidden depression in patients who have chronic complaints and who usually don't improve with medical treatment. People with migraines, muscle pain, chronic back pain, poly complainers or hypochondriacs (those who keep seeing doctors) can *mask* depression behind physical illnesses.

Depression is part of a group of psychiatric illnesses called **mood disorders**. One specific and well-known type is bipolar disorder. This is when a person can have depression or mania.

We call it mania when the mood swings upwards; depression when it swings downwards. *Mania,* for psychiatrists, means the following: the patient's mood swings, resulting in exaggerated energy, physical agitation, very rapid thinking and speech; they authorize themselves to do extravagant things, such as spending too much, drinking too much, having sex too much, sleeping too little, eating too little. This patient doesn't perceive themselves to be ill, so it's up to the family to take action. If the agitation and actions lead to reckless exposure, compulsory hospitalization may be indicated. In bipolar disorder, on the other hand, when the patient is depressed, treatment is easier because the person realizes they are ill and accepts help.

There are some people who go through life feeling a bit down, without much energy, spirit or enjoyment in the face of everyday events. They do their chores, they fulfill their obligations, but there's always something missing. It's as if they were carrying a burden, a weight on their back. If the person is religious, they run the risk of thinking that they are paying for some sin in life, so that later, in heaven, they can get their reward. In fact, we may be dealing with a type of chronic depression, called dysthymia - which can be treated with medication and psychotherapy.

Other external factors trigger depression. Alcohol is one of the biggest inducers of depression, as it is widely consumed, encouraged and consented to in our society. Alcohol is a substance that offers us alternatives for a happier life, with less inhibition and a sense of well-being. Whenever you drink, the first moments are of relief from anguish and sadness. Of course, this is a trap, as continued use can lead to addiction and mental illness. Remember that marijuana, cocaine, *crack* and psychoactive substances (such as *ecstasy*) also lead to depression and other mental illnesses, such as psychosis.

Chronic illnesses such as arthritis, diabetes, kidney failure, Parkinson's disease, diverticulitis, hepatitis, morbid obesity, stroke and myocardial infarction, among others, are also physical illnesses that can lead to depression.

* * *

In children, the disorder can reveal itself through loss of desire to play, fear of being away from their parents, unwillingness to go to school, difficulty staying in their own bed and sleeping, body and head aches, loss of urinary control at night and loss of appetite. In adolescents, depression can appear in the form of isolation, irritability, poor hygiene, school difficulties, weight loss or weight gain, alcohol or drug use and withdrawal from social activities.

Finally, in the elderly, the occurrence of depression increases due to the higher incidence of physical illnesses, side effects resulting from the use of many medications, the loss of loved ones and friends, increased economic difficulties, sensitivity due to family conflicts, social isolation and the presence of dementia symptoms.

There is also a special type of depression, which is puerperal depression, or postpartum depression. It can present itself in three different ways. The first is a mild, passing depression, called the *blues* (English slang for "depression", "sadness", "being down"); it occurs in 60% of women during their first pregnancy. Depressive symptoms usually appear soon after giving birth or, at most, within the first 15 days. It's a momentary sadness that gets better without treatment, just with family support.

In the second type of postpartum depression, the symptoms begin a fortnight after giving birth and are more severe, leaving the woman feeling low and unwilling to look after the baby. She becomes tearful, irritable, afraid of holding the child and hurting it; she loses sleep, doesn't want to breastfeed or sanitize the little one. In this case, psychotherapeutic approaches are necessary. There is also the possibility of taking antidepressants.

In the third and most serious type of puerperal depression, the mother has severe depressive symptoms: she can hear voices and even see the child in a distorted way. These are usually patients who already had mental problems before becoming pregnant. In these cases, the child must be kept away from the mother and medication must be used. Fortunately, this situation is not very common.

* * *

I want to focus on depression, which is closely linked to a person's existential experiences, their history, their traumas and their ghosts. It is a disorder caused or driven by conflicts, losses, separations and bereavements. Hardly anyone hasn't experienced trauma in their lifetime. Suffering childhood, harsh parents, marital conflicts, aggressive and disinterested children, loss of loved ones...

For some people, life or existential traumas can be significant, to the point of generating a depressive state. The danger in this case is that depression serves as an alibi to justify and perpetuate the lack of investment the person makes in the face of life's demands. These patients tend to explain away their suffering and blame it on negative past experiences. It becomes a vicious circle. *"I'm depressed because I suffered in the past and now I don't take care of my life because I'm depressed."* It becomes a snowball. It seems to be a "protective" depression, in the sense that the person doesn't take responsibility for looking after themselves because life has supposedly been bad for them.

Psychotherapy is essential for these depressive conditions, which are built on an emotional conflict, so that the patient can understand their traumas and resolve them. The use of antidepressants may also be indicated, but investing in medication alone may not bring good results.

* * *

Realize how important it is to diagnose depression. Many people are not properly diagnosed, even when they visit psychiatrists, psychologists, clinicians, gynecologists, neurologists and other specialists. It is also up to family members to keep an eye out for people who are close to them and who change their lifestyle, tending towards despondency, apathy, sadness, irritability and insomnia.

Untreated depression or depression treated without complete remission of symptoms will cause significant damage to the patient, as their quality of life will be very poor. Of course, the limitations will also appear in work performance, due to the frequent absence from work and the search for welfare benefits. In other words, public accounts are also affected by the depressive illness.

The most serious repercussion in the life of a depressed person is the risk of suicide. Teenagers and the elderly are the most susceptible to this extreme reaction. In a general comparison between men and women, although the rate of depression is much higher among women, they are the ones who commit suicide the most.

Faced with the fear that family members have that the patient might kill themselves, it is essential to talk about suicide. There is a fear among people in general that they won't talk about suicide with someone who is depressed. It's thought that this conversation could lead to the patient wanting to kill themselves. This is utter nonsense. On the contrary, it is essential to talk about this problem.

If you have someone close to you who is showing signs, who makes you suspect that there is a spark of suicide, act immediately, talk to them, make yourself available. Do it in a very simple, direct way, something like this: *"I want to talk to you about a concern that's on my mind. I imagine that you might want to end your life. Does my concern make sense?"*

If the depressed person answers yes, go on to talk about why they want to kill themselves. Tell them that the depression will pass, that their suffering is temporary, unlike death, which is forever or final. Make yourself available; say that if the bad ideas come back, they will seek your help. If the risk of suicide is intense, psychiatric hospitalization should be considered. Finally, it's always a good idea not to leave a firearm with someone who is depressed.

It's worth remembering that the treatment that offers the best and fastest results for a depressed person at risk of suicide is electroshock or electroconvulsive therapy. Don't be alarmed by the term. There are prejudices against this treatment; some uninformed people associate it with something medieval. It is used in extreme cases of suicide risk, carried out in hospital with the help of an anesthesiologist, meaning that the patient feels nothing. One or two applications can take the patient out of danger. When antidepressants are prescribed, they can take 20 to 30 days to have a positive effect. During this period, the risk of suicide is still present.

As you can see, the evil of the century is extremely dangerous, recurring and multifaceted. Let's always be on the lookout - for ourselves and for those around us.

THE PATHS OF EMOTIONAL ILLNESS

Regardless of culture, education, social level, beliefs and other characteristics, people in general have little knowledge, little intimacy with what goes on in the bowels of their emotional life or their unconscious. And the consequences of this are often imperceptible. While bodily illnesses, even the most sneaky and silent ones, can be detected through tests, emotional problems, on the other hand, generate reactions that can be mistaken for a physical illness, or that can even be ignored for a long time. Sooner or later, this ignorance can take its toll and show up in the form of limitations and damage caused by psychiatric symptoms.

Symptoms such as low mood, sadness, discouragement, lack of energy or bouts of crying are related to depression. Palpitation, sweating, shortness of breath, dizziness, fear and insomnia are linked to anxiety. These symptoms can stem from biochemical, cerebral or life-related problems, whether existential or psychological.

For didactic purposes, I'm dividing biological problems into emotional (or existential) ones. Firstly, I'm talking about psychiatric suffering of biological origin, related to a family history of illnesses, neurotransmitter deficiencies and genetic issues. Those who carry these natural predispositions can fall ill - regardless of whether their lives are good or bad. These are patients for whom the use of medication is indispensable.

In this text, however, I'm focusing on another group of people who suffer from mental illness linked to day-to-day conflicts, to unresolved issues that lead to suffering. It is therefore essential that we talk about the paths to emotional illness, about this road that we pave ourselves and which leads directly to suffering.

It's difficult to quantify, but I realize from my experience that many psychiatric problems stem from the "emotional traps" that people develop throughout their lives. As I said, there are inevitable psychic problems, the result of genetic predispositions. But in general, the problems are of our own making. Here are some examples of these traps.

* * *

A lady has been constantly devoting herself to an older friend, to the point where, in order to keep her company, she has given up going out for the summer and going for walks with her relatives. The person she cares for intensely is demanding and always asks for more care. The volunteer caregiver suggests that her sick friend go to a relative's house for better care, but her suggestion is not accepted. The caregiver then starts to have problems such as loss of sleep, anxiety and depression.

Clearly, this was her unconscious way of allowing herself to distance herself from her castrating and demanding friend. Her emotional illness turned out to be a *necessary evil*, a constructed alibi. In this case, psychotherapy is important to help clarify the unconscious reasons for the illness. In the case of our example, medication would be of little benefit. The important thing is to understand the underlying conflicts that led to this path.

As you can see, the emotional problems of the vast majority of people are actually unconscious decisions that have led them down tortuous and rocky roads. Their relationships, their expressions of feelings, their exchanges of experiences, in short, much of what they have done, constitutes the sidewalk that ends up in the situation of suffering.

* * *

A young man from a humble background was going on his first trip abroad with his girlfriend. His parents were indignant and showed their annoyance at not being invited on the trip. The son became very nervous about the conflict that had arisen. Suddenly, he began to feel nervous, his chest tightened, his heart raced, he was afraid of dying and other symptoms linked to panic disorder. As a result, he lost the courage to travel and canceled the trip.

Notice the presence of mental illness as a decisive factor. The son panicked and was soon no longer able to make decisions or travel. He didn't have to contradict his parents. It's clear that the patient here ends up punishing himself above all by unconsciously giving up his trip. It wasn't really him who decided not to travel, but his anxiety symptoms that decided for him.

* * *

When the body is ill, there are basically two symptoms that help us identify the situation and seek help: pain and fever. When the mind is ill, different signals are also emitted, in two groups of symptoms: those linked to depression and those linked to anxiety.

Both physical and mental symptoms are welcome. Realize that feeling bad, down or distressed can be good, as long as you seek help. An inappropriate alternative is to combat suffering through the use of alcohol, marijuana, synthetic drugs, cocaine or tranquilizers (black belt type). The time has come to leave the erratic road and look for another one that will lead to a less painful path.

The best way to resolve these emotional problems is through psychotherapy. Empathy with the therapist is fundamental to the success of this method.

The damage that emotional conflicts cause in many different areas is quite visible. One example is sex life. The causes of erection or orgasm difficulties are rarely physical or hormonal. The bulk of the problems are emotional. Taking Viagra can therefore produce very limited results.

The road metaphor is very valid here. Imagine a car being driven along a dark, bumpy road with various hazards. Inevitably, the vehicle will break down. You can proceed with repairs, such as changing a flat tire, but the road will continue to be inhospitable and, sooner or later, further breakdowns will occur. It's the same with emotional or psychological problems. The person who takes the wrong road may resort to medication that relieves their pain for a while, but the depths of their suffering will remain intact and at any moment they will develop new illnesses or those that already seemed to have been overcome will flare up. What hinders the driver here is the fact that, on his own, he can't realize that he needs to change his route. I'm referring here to the need for help from a psychotherapist.

It's important to reiterate that psychiatry today has an arsenal of really important and useful medications. I'm saying this so you don't think I'm giving more importance to psychotherapy over the use of medication. Medication for some psychiatric illnesses is fundamental, preventing relapses and psychiatric hospitalizations.

THE TRIGGER THAT SETS OFF PANIC DISORDER

Today, a psychiatric disorder called *panic* disorder is well known. The name comes from the god Pan in Greek mythology. He has the ears, horns and legs of a goat, but the rest of his body is human. Pan used to scare people, especially those who walked through the woods at night. When the entity was present, the victims became anxious, as if they had been given a fright. Panic disorder was named after this mythological character.

Anxiety is the great villain of this pathology, and the person is suddenly affected by physical and psychological symptoms resulting from this anxiety. Fainting, weakness, dizziness, a feeling that the head is swollen, a racing heart, a tight chest, sweating and difficulty breathing. Patients report a fear of going mad and imminent death. It is difficult for someone who has never experienced something like this to understand what is happening.

Faced with this crisis, the patient rushes to the nearest emergency medical service. There they are examined and sent home after a thorough assessment. They are given a tranquilizer and calm down. Doctors usually don't notice anything abnormal from a physical or cardiological point of view.

This patient, at first, doesn't agree that the basis of their problem could be of psychiatric or psychological origin. He continues to think that it is a heart problem and that he will die suddenly. When faced with other crises, they follow the same path. In hospitals, he is advised to see a psychiatrist, but he is reluctant because there is a lot of prejudice against the idea of suffering from a mental problem.

If they don't seek specialized help, they run the risk of having a second problem. They may develop fears or phobias and start to avoid the places where they had anxiety attacks, resulting in a restriction of the spaces they used to go to. Phobias generate anticipatory fears and anxieties, i.e. just the thought of being in a certain place makes the person nervous. The fear can grow to the point where the person needs to be monitored even in their own home, for fear of suffering an attack alone and dying. Bad disease!

When people finally think of seeing a psychiatrist, they usually go begrudgingly. They always hope for a magic remedy that will solve everything quickly. The aim of this article is to introduce you, the reader, to a dark and secret world, so that you can better understand the labyrinths of panic disorder.

I'll illustrate with the story of a very intelligent young woman with a university degree and great potential for success in the face of life's demands. After finishing her university degree, with a master's and a doctorate, she passed a public examination and ended up moving to another state to work as a university professor. She told me about experiences that were typical of panic disorder, including seeking out hospitals and undergoing tests that detected nothing. She was put on medication and the crises became less intense, although they were still present.

I was very curious to know under what circumstances her first crisis had occurred. She recalled that her first episode of panic had occurred shortly after moving to another city, when her parents were visiting. It was the first time she had received them in her new home. Her mother was a very demanding and authoritarian woman, who acted as if she was the only one who knew the right way to do everything. "Fussy" and "opinionated" - that's how the young woman described her mother. The mother didn't make it professionally, but she placed herself in the family's life as if she knew the best ways to go about it. It was clear that her daughter was capable and competent in the face of life's demands, but her mother didn't think so. She always criticized her daughter's attitudes. The father was also successful professionally, but the mother often disqualified him.

When she welcomed her parents to their new home, she made sure to give them her best. She tidied up the house, the room they would be staying in, organized programs, visits around the city, restaurants, meetings with friends, etc. Despite being extremely competent in her activities, from an emotional point of view, she felt fragile, as she needed her mother's confirmation to really recognize herself as capable. One night, a situation arose in which her mother disqualified her from her father and husband. That morning, the patient woke up feeling panicked, mobilized the whole family and ended up in hospital for treatment. The second crisis occurred six months later, days before her parents were due to visit her in Europe, where she was studying.

I understand that this situation of needing her mother's agreement on her performance left this girl feeling disempowered in the face of life. In other words, her mother was the guarantor of her competence, but she didn't offer her daughter any words of comfort. I think the panic attacks had a protective meaning!

"*How can a psychic illness be protective?*" is the obvious and automatic question that comes to the reader's mind. I'll explain. It's something protective in relation to the great irritation that was occurring and that she feared externalizing, putting out and attacking her mother with contained anger, which could have serious consequences. In this way, the panic attack sapped her strength and she was weakened to the point of needing help from others.

It could be said that these crises were the girl's fault, because they prevented something worse from happening. For the imaginary mother-daughter duo, it was like a confirmation of the daughter's incompetence, pushing the mother to get more and more involved in the girl's life. And she responded by getting *sick*. She continued to take medication. She improved when she began to understand the unconscious conflicts that led to her symptoms. Psychotherapy brings to consciousness the feelings that lie in the rubble of the mind and cause damage.

Realize that if this illness were purely physical-chemical, it would appear randomly - not in situations of strong pent-up emotions. It would occur in the most diverse situations and contexts. The case I'm using as an example reveals something contrary to the chemical origin. It's not suffering that appears at random: we have a pattern, with panic attacks always being caused by the same reasons. In other words, pure emotion! The triggering factors come from outside, they work like a trigger that fires a projectile that hits the patient's mind, causing the symptoms. Medicines alone do not stop this cycle.

I remembered another situation that happened on a flight I was taking from France to Brazil. I was talking to a passenger next to me; when he found out that I was a psychiatrist, he told me that he was worried about a good friend of his. This friend no longer wanted to work as an employee, he wanted to start his own business, but his wife wouldn't accept it. The friend begrudgingly went along with his wife's wishes. What happened next?

The friend's reaction to his wife's imposition was to rebel internally. How? By having panic attacks when he got to work. In this way, he had the "unconscious alibi" of not staying where, after all, he didn't want to be. According to this flight companion, his friend had taken various medications, but to no avail. After a while, I took the liberty of saying: "I don't think your friend is going to get better by taking medication. He first needs to resolve the conflict with his wife, to whom he is submitting."

Perhaps the young man was afraid to admit his desire, at the risk of losing his love and even his wife's company. Well, we've arrived in Brazil and I don't know if he's taken these considerations of mine to his distressed friend...

Perhaps there are good drugs for this illness; drugs that reduce anxiety and make life less painful. Psychiatrists first learn to use this resource in their training, because it's the easiest to teach.

Developing the art of working in psychotherapy and psychoanalysis is the most difficult part of training these professionals. Many psychiatric illnesses are triggered by emotional or psychological conflicts, in other words, they are responsible for the illness. In these cases, psychotherapy as a form of help is fundamental. Medical statistics confirm that the use of medication and psychotherapy brings the best results.

LEADER OR BOSS

This is a complex and difficult subject. How can anyone know how to shape a good leader? I say this because, in fact, it is more complex and laborious to be a leader than to hold a position or function as a director, CEO, manager or boss.

The boss exercises a received power and relies exclusively on this, commanding through pressure, the power he exercises, using clear or veiled threats, imposition and constraint. All in the name of achieving the company's objectives. In a tribe, the chief is usually the strongest, the one who imposes the most fear on the group; he is the most truculent and punishes physically if necessary.

When we hear a news item on TV about criminal factions, we hear about the head of the faction, the powerful guy. Therefore, the word boss suggests a guy in charge and not someone who seeks out his targets, using other skills to achieve his goals. The word **boss** comes from the French "*chieef*" and the Latin "*caput*", which means "head", the one who is above and at the head of everything. But we don't have to take the meaning of this word literally.

In one way or another, at some point in our lives, each of us has to make decisions and lead people. Let's start with the most common example: the role of parent. Here you can already see the difference between a leader and a boss.

Parents who listen to their children, even the little ones, who talk to them before making a decision, who don't use their economic power to oppress them, in short, parents who are less bossy and abusive, are more aligned with leaders.

Despotic parents, on the other hand, put it like this: "I'm in charge here!"; "Those who can are in charge, those who have to obey"; "I pay the bills, so I decide"; "Let those who are uncomfortable leave"; "I'm the head of the family". What can we expect from this parent profile within an organization?

Probably, this aspect that appears at home will be similar to the performance within a company.

Another example: the role of teacher. Sometimes, teachers aren't prepared for the job and hide behind an arrogant posture, compatible with that of a boss, so as not to be held to account by their students. Poor students will suffer for the rest of their lives. Ignorance, a lack of knowledge, fragility - all this encourages the so-called role of boss, as he will try to protect his weaknesses using the shield of the powerful. In this way, he keeps the student at a distance, with no room for pressure.

Well, we need people taking on managerial tasks, exercising some kind of command, making decisions about company strategies and the lives of employees. I'm talking about CEOs, directors, supervisors, coordinators, managers, in short, those who coordinate people in corporate environments. They are the ones who make decisions, determine actions, outline strategies and seek performance. Unlike relationships between friends and family, here there isn't the natural empathy of an affinity bond, which can make the task easier.

In the world of work, the boss always has to prove that he deserves his position. And this intermittent proof must be offered to those above him, to the directors, so that they keep him in the job and give him credit before the others. And it must also be given to those below, the subordinates, so that they produce and help the manager achieve the objectives expected by the corporation.

If employees perceive that they have to obey and follow someone who is incapable of leading, the organizational project will be compromised. And this possible incapacity is usually not only linked to professional deficiencies, i.e. a lack of technical knowledge on the part of the decision-maker. The biggest obstacle to good leadership lies in the coordinator's inability to perceive more subjective or emotional aspects, both his own and those of the group. The boss doesn't care about listening to the other person - he makes the decision and that's that. And herein lies a major difference between these two types of managers: the true ability to listen before deciding.

True leadership is exercised through a direct posture and attitude. Straight talking, no half words, clearly showing your likes and dislikes, being able to listen to your peers' and subordinates' disagreements, exercising an authority granted by others, not an imposed power.

The leader sees himself as just another member of the team, but without forgetting to share in the responsibilities, the duties and, above all, the successes. They know how to talk and listen, and take into account what others have to say about projects, objectives, relationships, in short, everything that concerns the work they are involved in.

A competent leader asks more questions to get to the point they want to make, leaving aside confrontation, inquisition, talk, gossip, threats or illusions. Have you noticed that, with good questioning, our interlocutor shows us, step by step, what he thinks, how he acts, giving us the path we need to follow?

In fact, the leader goes beyond the professional relationship and shows a real interest in the lives of his subordinates. After all, a work team spends more time together than a family usually does. Really getting to know your employees is more important than you might think, because then you know how to deal with them, because you know what kind of expectations you can create, how to help them and be helped, in short. With closer ties, relationships become clearer, people become more trustworthy and everyone has a better time at work. Realizing that an employee is not doing well emotionally, giving yourself permission to talk to them about this perception and making yourself available to talk will generate a lot of trust.

In addition, it is essential for the leader to find out what the team thinks of him. Of course, it's not the most natural thing in the world for an employee to openly tell their director or manager what they think of them. Rather, there needs to be a build-up, a display of genuine openness on the part of the leader, inspiring trust and showing that they will listen to complaints or criticism.

Since it's not easy to say directly what you think of a coordinator, it would be interesting to make ballot boxes available for employees to put their opinions in, without having to sign them. This opens up a way for the manager to know what they think of him or her.

With actions like these, everyone wins. It's only fair that companies want the best results. Perhaps by using imposing and authoritarian bosses, they will achieve their goals for a short period of time. However, by putting real leaders in charge of their employees, the organization will reap lasting rewards and will not only leave its customers satisfied, but also its employees.

* * *

I was recently in São Luís do Maranhão. By the hotel swimming pool, I saw the waiter wearing a long-sleeved black shirt, black pants and dress shoes. He was sweating excessively and seemed very upset about his working conditions. You don't have to think very hard, you don't have to have an MBA in personnel management or specialize in fashion *design* to know that closed, hot clothes shouldn't be the uniform of someone who serves people in the sun, at temperatures always above 30 degrees. Since I'm an observer and like to share my ideas, I spoke to the management of this hotel about my perception. I noticed that I was dealing with a boss, not a leader, as he gave me some bureaucratic explanations, indicating that he didn't care much about the waiters.

Providing good working conditions for staff is the primary role of a good leader. And treating employees well is a moral obligation of companies which, if not fulfilled, not only shows a lack of humanity, but also a lack of intelligence (if we consider the damage, even involuntary, that dissatisfied employees can cause). It is by observing the way you relate to your employees that we can see who is who in the corporate world.

It's interesting to see how productivity targets are created in companies. People will always respond positively to these targets, even if they haven't been discussed with employees. But in the long run, they will succumb to exhaustion, because the target was created in the head of the boss, without any complicity with those who are going to achieve it.

Leaders don't create distance between their subordinates. Although he is in a senior role, he relates as an equal, even with lower-ranking employees.

He doesn't need barriers, he has contact with everyone - and without having to play the people's *friend*.

The personality of those who drive makes all the difference. The *obsessive* person locks everything away, gets lost in details and nit-picking. The apathetic and sad person, with depressive traits, won't have the energy to invest in projects and relationships. The *impulsive* person is bossy, controlling, gets irritated by any setback and can lose everything. The *phobic* is afraid of taking risks, thinks everything could go wrong, finds it difficult to get close to people and can become anxious. The *paranoid,* due to their distrust of everything and everyone, does not allow themselves to be close and complicit with the group. The *addict* doesn't commit to their projects because they need everyone to agree with them.

* * *

Finally. We need technical competence, knowledge, skill and study to climb the ranks within organizations. However, we will only be able to reach higher levels and stay there if we are mentally healthy. Therefore, being a leader or a boss requires the ability to deal well with your own emotions, to be able to understand a little about the emotions of your employees and, if possible, to know how to manage them. The boss won't have these skills, these *feelings,* unlike the leader.

The good thing about this whole conversation is that our characteristics and ways of relating are changeable. We need to believe that and change what we need to.

POWER, POTENCY AND THE WHEEL OF FORTUNE

There is a medieval figure of speech known as the wheel of fortune. It is a representation of the different stages we go through in life. "Fortune", in this case, is fate, luck. Sometimes the wheel is up, sometimes it's down. The cantata Carmina Burana represents this well. Its first movement, known worldwide - *O Fortuna, Imperatrix Mundi* - is very explicit in narrating how human life is a succession of joys and miseries, joys and sorrows. Its first stanza, freely translated from Latin, goes like this:

"O, luck, / you are like the moon / changeable, / always growing, / or shrinking; / detestable life / sometimes oppresses / and sometimes relieves, / the mind just for fun. / Poverty, / power, / dissolve like ice."

Who doesn't want visibility? Who doesn't want to be recognized, valued, have money, important friends and be honored? We all do. We all want people to admit that we're good at what we do, for the social context to give us the value we think we deserve. This is natural, it's part of our essence. We tend to invest in concrete, external values, which in our culture are highly prized. However, there is another way of investing: in personal, internal, subjective values, which are not very admired or coveted. Faced with this duality, I would like to introduce the vision of power and potency.

Power is made up of elements outside of us, external, which may belong to us, but in a transitory, passing way. The job you have, the salary you earn, social relationships centered on interests, the goods you own, the trips you take, the beautiful woman you show off, your muscular and "healed" body. In short, these are all situations that we may or may not experience, but which are external, giving us power, *status* and notoriety. Public applause, appearances on radio and television programs, political office... Conditions that we all like and crave. And when we achieve them, we feel enormous satisfaction.

However, we must always bear in mind that we are talking about temporary situations. We tend to forget the ephemeral nature of power, because we get intoxicated by the gains, by the joy of conquest, by the feeling of appreciation it offers us. We can see this clearly in political circles. From councillors to the President of the Republic, including MPs, governors and ministers, it is very common to come across people who are intoxicated by the power they hold, forgetting that the wheel of fortune turns endlessly. And this is common because these people who are attached to power don't pay enough attention to other aspects that do make a difference to those who cultivate them. And they can be summed up in what I call **power**.

Power is internal, personal and non-transferable. These are values and achievements that lie within each one of us - and they will remain there, regardless of whether recognition comes or not.

For example: if I've studied a lot, acquired culture, advanced in my erudition, worked hard, all these acts will result in achievements, in personal progress. In other words, they will be powers within me. Other experiences that greatly enhance us: our ability to make true friends, to show our affection, to be generous, attentive, loving, tolerant and respectful. In other words, truly caring about others, regardless of social class, wealth, color, race, religion; how close we can get to someone who is sick or dying, and how much we can intercede on behalf of someone who is suffering some kind of *bullying* or aggression.

Nowadays, powers have taken a back seat. We see a society that is very power-oriented. We have abandoned **being** and prioritized **having** and - even worse - **seeming**.

In fact, this is a noticeable change. For a long time now, powers have been neglected in favor of powers, but there has been a recent phenomenon of increasing superficiality. As people are taking on responsibilities later and later in life, and in a context of online, excessively virtual lives, not even power has really been won. People have become increasingly content with merely appearing to have power. If it used to be important to flaunt material achievements around, in the - let's say - real world, now it's enough to give the impression, via the internet, that we are someone, that we have, that we possess.

Intimacy and complicity with those close to us is a differential that generates power. We see relationships becoming increasingly distant and empty. Families don't share feelings, affections, information and time. Everyone has their own virtual world, and the priority is contact with this make-believe world. Friends exchange almost ciphered words through messages on apps. We have lost the ability to read, reflect and express ourselves, because Google offers us everything.

Even dating has been practiced in a virtual way. At some point, virtual lovers meet and exchange secretions through kissing and sexual intercourse. Immediately, they return to the refuge of virtuality, where their exposure is masked by the *fake* characters they* that they build up.

We must therefore bear in mind that we have invested a lot in power, which makes us shine in the eyes of others. I don't think it's bad or critical to seek to make money and have power. However, I emphasize that focusing only on this path can generate a feeling of emptiness, which will grow in proportion to the increase in power and money.

In this scenario of discouragement, the risk of using alcohol and other drugs increases, as does an unbridled quest to have sex with more and more people, partying almost daily, spending astronomical amounts of money, gambling, etc. But none of this will bring well-being and inner peace. Then we see the development of depression, anxiety attacks, phobias, panic disorder, insomnia, loss of sexual libido or impotence. This is what is known as post-modernity, where everything is gaseous and evaporates quickly.

I find it very difficult for people to be with themselves, in the sense of reading a book, a newspaper, a magazine, going to the movies, reflecting, in short, developing the ability to fill themselves up at certain moments in their lives. Human beings are solitary, in the sense that whenever they make a decision, it is their decision alone, it is a solitary act. I think that a good way to develop our power further is through this appropriation.

---

* Editor's note: from the English, fake; used, in the virtual context, to characterize characters that people create to interact online.

Think of the Carmina Burana cantata, the wheel of fortune, luck, fate, spinning up and down. I think we can reduce the risk of the influence of fate, of luck, by the way each of us builds our lives.

D.R. - DISCUSSING THE RELATIONSHIP

Think about marital relationships, dating, *affairs*, in short, the bonds between couples. How many hours have you and your partners, today and in the past, wasted in endless arguments? Many, many hours - that's my bet. And I'm betting big.

D.R., the acronym for *relationship discussion*, is the modern name for this endless circular movement of inextricable quarrels and disagreements. We start by talking about a specific problem, move on to another, and another, pulling the thread of an endless ball of yarn. Before you know it, you can't even remember the beginning of the discussion, the central object of the conversation. We quickly tend to fall into a scheme of accusation and justification - our mistakes or difficulties are all explainable; the other person's are all unforgivable.

In the **art of being unhappy**, the central theme of this book, one of the main skills is that of wasting time and energy on discussions that will lead nowhere. Or they might, but it will be a very different place to the one we imagined when we started the conversation. Frustration, anger, resentment, a desire for revenge and distancing oneself from the other are the most common results.

I like to see couples and families in my work, and these meetings are usually successful, with no fights or accusations. However, I have ended a consultation with a couple because of this. They had barely started to talk about their problems and they were already arguing insanely, one accusing the other, in the loudest and most confusing way imaginable.

As a spectator, I witnessed what we've all experienced: the parties in a relationship trying to impose their way of doing things and taking serious offense. In the case I'm sharing here, I thought it best to interrupt our meeting, as I was "dizzy" and anxious in the midst of that D.R. - and I had no power to calm them down. I, who was on the outside, succumbed, I was knocked out watching that clash; imagine who is in the scene, on stage, as the protagonist.

What I perceive in these moments of discussion is that they are impregnated with a vice of origin: whoever proposes the discussion usually wants to impose their way of seeing things on the other. This is therefore an exercise in power, in force. "*Let's see who gives in at the end, who falls to their knees and retracts and apologizes!*"

Here I describe a concept that you have already seen and will see in various passages of this book: the **desire for control**. It manifests itself in this R.D. context as discussions that aren't frank conversations, in which we share with the other person a situation that has occurred and that hasn't done us any good, expecting them to respond with their view. What can hide behind this apparent dialog is that someone wants to impose their will, their reason and their convictions. It's an imposition of their thinking on the other person's head. This desire for control is present in the emotional or unconscious state of many people, and it comes out in a constant and impulsive way (even if it is often disguised as a desire to help, to do good). The worst thing is that the person who harbors these feelings has no conscious awareness that they are doing so.

These difficulties are not only related to the couple's intimate and subjective life. They can extend to any topic in everyday life. Politics, soccer, religion, clothing, leisure, raising children, etc. We tend to impose our will and our beliefs on the other person's head. We are always "right". And this is where the danger lies. Sometimes we even use threats to achieve our goals: "I'm going to split up", "I'm not going to have sex with you anymore", "I'm going to talk to your parents", "I'm going to tell our children", "I'm going to sleep in another room".

Some people don't have the ability to express what they feel and think. In these cases, they tend to fight, shout and swear when they offer their disagreements. If the other partner is more competent and perceptive, they can try to calm them down by saying: "*This isn't a nice way to go, there's a risk that*

I'll start verbally attacking you too. Maybe we can stop our conversation here and try to resume it tomorrow?"

We must bear in mind that when we ponder and put forward our points of view in any everyday conversation, our psychic *modus operandi* will appear. In other words, aspects of our personality will give a darker or lighter color to the course of the conversation. I emphasize that the rational and logical aspects can take a back seat, which is complicated. What to do, if that's how we work?

Why do we want to be right or come out looking like winners in a conversation with someone who is intimate, a partner, an accomplice, a lover and dear to us? I think that this imposing way of relating hides feelings of insecurity, fragility, mistrust, fears and obsessive thoughts. This type of person needs the other person to agree with their arguments, so that they have a temporary feeling that they are more valued and loved. Soon, however, all the conflicts will return - and the cycle of unhealthy R.D. begins all over again.

If you're looking for emotional well-being, try to avoid the pitfalls that discussing your relationship can lead to, because anyone who wants a certain harmony in a relationship should know that the meaning of a relationship is the diversity of thinking, speaking and positioning oneself and, for this, it's essential to be able to disagree, to see the world differently from the other.

If you notice that you're getting angry with your partner, that's a good reason to stop the conversation. Tell him or her that this conversation is hurting you, because you perceive inner discomfort and anger. Gently suggest interrupting and returning to the subject another day.

Another pertinent thought. If you notice someone starting to repeat the same text, the same phrases and arguments, it's a warning sign to stop. This discussion will be repetitive, tiresome and annoying. So get out of it and try to come back another day. Note that I say another day! Yes, you can wait to talk, there's time and it's even healthy to put it off, as it may reduce the anger, if there is any. Tell your partner: "Look, you've already said that, you're being repetitive, and I'm losing interest in this conversation."

I also don't think it's a good idea to discuss things late at night, as there's a risk of creating anxiety in the couple, to the point where they lose sleep, which is very bad. We mustn't forget that the next day awaits us with open arms for our usual activities and, if we're tired, we run the risk of getting in the way.

Imagine a productive ending for a D.R.! What would that be like? Something like this:

- I didn't realize it upset you!

- I'll think about it carefully.

- I'm glad you said that, I didn't think it would be a problem.

- I don't agree with you, but I'll think about it and we'll talk again!

- I think it's good that you spoke out, but your way of expressing yourself could have been less aggressive.

- We don't have to think the same way, but I think it's good that we don't go into this subject any more, as it leads to suffering.

- Let's not discuss anything when one of us has been drinking!

- I was inappropriate and rude to you, I didn't like my attitude! Life goes on, let's keep taking care of ourselves!

- I realized my mistake, I'm sorry, I ran over you in the conversation with friends, I'll try not to repeat it.

Much better, no? Bet big that the results will be different from those we're used to in the D.R.

DON'T BE AFRAID OF OTHER PEOPLE'S OPINIONS

We all want to be accepted, to receive applause and recognition. In the idealized world of our egos, we would like our jokes and witticisms to be the funniest; our opinions, the most considered and respected; our actions, the most revered. However, this is clearly not how the band plays, how life goes. In fact, more often than not it isn't.

So we have a couple of options. Either we shrug off the fact that the world doesn't embrace us all the time, or we become excessively preoccupied with it, losing peace of mind and naturalness in our actions, always worried about how people will receive our attitudes; or we observe other people's opinions with attention and respect, absorb what works for us and discard the rest, without it bothering us.

Well, it's fundamental for our emotional balance to oxygenate our minds, so that we can expose ourselves, show what's going on in our heads using words or actions.

Fear of other people's opinions of us can become a recurring phobia in our times, when **having** and - above all - **appearing** are more important than **being**. We've ended up becoming a society full of *Marias vain as hell.* I'm referring to the expression used to characterize people with weak personalities, who follow others rather than their own convictions.

Today we tend to live in a politically correct style, in other words, we follow behaviors and act in line with the group that surrounds us.

With the advent of virtual media, the individuality of thinking and acting seems to have been crushed by the mass of internet users who are furious at those who stray from the herd. A model of external control over the thinking and acting of others has been created, in the style of George Orwell's *1984*. It's incredible to see that something written in 1948 and thought to have happened in 1984 is still so true, so current. It's not the story, it's the consequences, the fears, the surveillance, the control, the truths told as lies and vice versa, the absolute power of one or a few people, the manipulation.

This literary classic is sensational. It's a dystopia in which, in a totalitarian society, Winston, the protagonist, lives a regulated life, commanded and watched by Big Brother - the ever-present eye of the oppressive state, which sees everything, through mechanisms spread everywhere.

Dystopias are generally characterized by totalitarianism, authoritarianism and oppressive control of society. In them, the curtains fall and society is revealed to be corruptible; the rules created for the common good are shown to be flexible. Technology is used as a tool to control both the state and institutions - or even corporations. Based on the book, the well-known *reality* TV *show* Big Brother was created, in which everyone and everything is controlled through cameras placed in every space, except the toilets.

But for a more fulfilling, satisfying and creative life, we need to detach ourselves from the *big brother* we've planted in our minds, because it's from our imagination that we give strength to what others would think about us, taking up too much of other people's impressions and becoming *Marias que vão com* as *outras*.

I don't mean that we should be selfish, inconsequential, that we simply don't care about other people's feelings and impressions. What we should do is not let other people's opinions of us shape the way we are, the way we act, the way we think. Respect others, always; submit to others, never.

It is appropriate and sensible to pay attention to words, opinions and even criticism. It's quite likely that if we give constructive criticism due consideration, we can benefit from it. On the other hand, we must be attentive to the content of the opinions of those who give them to us, because they are often just empty condemnations and judgments, based on hasty and inattentive impressions, or even pure envy or spite. For fear of other people's opinions, we cannot stop being who we are and act according to our wills and inclinations.

The great danger surrounding those who keep quiet because of other people's opinions is that they use this artifice to effectively avoid committing themselves to the adult and responsible care of their lives. It can be an unconscious alibi to use someone else's opinion to avoid taking responsibility for their own thinking, hoping that things will settle down as they *go* along. This alibi will only harm those who are seduced by it. Exposing your thoughts, feelings and actions is a great source of energy for boosting your esteem, security and confidence in the face of life's impositions on you.

I often hear things like: *"I didn't say what I thought because I was afraid of the other person's reaction"*. Well, we don't have the slightest ability to know what the other person will think, what their reaction will be. The rest is an exercise in futurology. Of course, whenever you offer your ideas or take action, do so with respect and politeness.

Not being clear can be very damaging in all areas of life. How many times have you failed to offer an idea in your workplace because you were afraid that your proposal wouldn't be accepted? Perhaps you've stopped asking someone out because you were afraid of the response to your invitation. Or you've stopped wearing an outfit for fear of oblique, condemning glances! You didn't want to disagree with your partner for fear of being left. On a night out, you've stopped trying to approach a potentially interesting companion for fear of not being accepted... And so on.

Be careful not to become immobilized in your life! Don't use others to justify your paralysis. Don't let yourself be guided by others. Try to show yourself, to offer yourself. Don't shy away from giving your opinion, making jokes, presenting ideas, being who you are. As Nietzsche said, "amor fati" - in other words, like and enjoy things as they are; in this case, like who you are.

The safe harbor we can reach would be the one where we allow ourselves to be truthful and transparent and, on the other hand, also develop the ability and competence to listen to what the other person has to say to us, even if they say it in a way that hurts our ears. On the other hand, it is neither wise nor recommended that we take offense at what we are told, even if we don't agree with what we hear.

The other day, a patient said that she feared she would get worse or be harmed by a medication I had prescribed. Of course, I didn't feel disqualified by her statement. I realized that it revealed her insecurities and mistrust of the people who were trying to help her. She had a history of childhood abuse from her parents, those who were supposed to look after her. I was just someone who was trying to look after her. In her imagination, the fear of abuse was present.

The art of being unhappy develops with vigor in this fertile ground, which is fear and the consequent paralysis resulting from looking at and thinking about others.

SOMATIZATION – WHEN THE BODY SPEAKS FOR US

The term somatization is translated from the Germanic word *Organsprache,* which literally means the "speech of the organs". It is a concept created by Wilhelm Stekel (who was close to Freud) at the beginning of the 20th century. The term could represent both physical manifestations with organic lesions and physical symptoms with no medical explanation, as long as they were generated by unconscious psychological conflicts.

At the end of the 20th century, the definition of somatization turned mainly to unexplained physical symptoms, abandoning the concept of physical illnesses of psychic origin, the so-called psychosomatic illnesses.

When our emotional suffering, our conflicts, are so strong that they transcend the psyche, we see consequences for our physical health. This is what is known as somatization. In a nutshell, it's when the **art of being unhappy** has taken over our being in such a way that the body also pays the bill.

Realize that the body and mind have an umbilical connection of intense intimacy. In other words, the person is subjected to some emotional suffering, but it's the body that shows the discomfort. This is somatization. The body also speaks through symptoms. It's still an outlet created by our mind, by our imagination, in the face of unbearable pressures that pass through our unconscious.

Imagine a person suffering from anguish, with no idea where this discomfort comes from. Transforming unconscious psychological suffering into something tangible, like a physical problem, is a reasonable alternative to the imaginary. In this way, we have something to treat that shows its face through physical symptoms.

Headaches, gastritis, nausea, muscle or back pain, shortness of breath, rapid heartbeat, high blood pressure, dermatitis, asthma, autoimmune diseases, loss of voice, vaginal pain during sex, difficulty getting an erection... In short, the manifestations of somatization are many. The important thing here is to be very clear: many people become physically ill as a result of emotional issues. Our daily anxieties and conflicts amplify our problems, making our bodies sick.

I like to make the analogy between body and mind. When we have an illness exclusively of the body, there are often two symptoms that are essential for us to seek help: fever and pain. When the mind gets sick, there are also two strands of symptoms that signal that we need help: depression and anxiety.

* * *

There is a disease that is present, fibromyalgia. In my opinion, this is an example of somatization. The person suffers from pain all over the body, which changes location and is accompanied by low mood, irritability, etc. There are no laboratory or imaging tests that indicate any cause for this pathology. We treat this illness with the same drugs we prescribe for depression and anxiety. I've accompanied several patients with these symptoms, all of whom had very significant emotional triggers. That being said, it's clear that medication alone may not be enough to help and that psychotherapeutic support is needed. In this case, psychotherapy helps to clarify the patient's imagination, bringing to consciousness the conflicts that triggered the fibromyalgia and thus alleviating the suffering.

I'll give you another family example. My mother (now deceased) felt sick to her stomach when she ate at night. Italian families in the countryside of Rio Grande do Sul developed the habit of having coffee with milk for dinner, along with other foods such as salami, cheese, eggs and even steak cooked on the wood-burning stove. Although she ate all this variety of heavy food, she didn't think she was *having* dinner; she thought she was just *having coffee*, a "reinforced" *coffee*. However, if she went to a restaurant, or even to her son's house, to eat any hot dish, as filling as her "coffee", she would get sick to her stomach. Even though I was a psychiatrist, I couldn't help her with this somatization. "Saints don't work miracles," says the popular wisdom. In fact, she didn't worry too much about her nocturnal food intolerance; I think we children took more notice.

Another memory that comes to mind: patients who go to their doctor's appointments often have high blood pressure at the time, but when they return home, it normalizes.

Another: a lady said that everything she ate attacked her liver. The liver is to blame for so many things! She felt bloated and had occasional diarrhea. Even drinking water could hurt her. She was always going to the doctor, sure that something would happen. However, all the specialists she went to were unanimous in telling her - backed up by tests and analyses - that she had no physical illness. Despite this, she swore she could see the symptoms of the illnesses she claimed to be suffering from. After wandering around the clinics, she was sent for a psychiatric assessment - which she didn't like, because she didn't think she was *crazy*.

As we talked, she came to understand that all her fears were not based on reality, but on anxieties that she herself had created. She was in a difficult situation at work, because she didn't agree with the attitudes of her father, who owned the company and with whom she feared disagreeing. She feared his explosive reaction and also the unknown reaction she might have. She began to realize what was behind her somatization and that, if she followed this path, there was a good chance that she would soon end up getting really sick.

What happened to this patient is exemplary. The moment she was free of her anxieties, her body stopped "talking", stopped giving physical signs of her psychic distress. Her connection with her unconscious anxieties, which came to light in psychotherapy, led her to improve her physical complaints. She was able to replace her physical symptoms with conversations with her father. Neither her father went mad nor did she have to fight with him.

* * *

In time: it's worth providing some medical information about the liver. It's one of the most capable and competent organs in our body and, although it doesn't get sick very often, it always takes the blame for symptoms whose causes are unknown.

If we have a conflict, an upset, and we don't realize it, we end up with some kind of suffering. This can manifest itself in the form of irritation, anxiety or whatever; or it can end up "bursting out" in the body. That's why it's essential that we have a strong intimacy with our emotional life, so that we can understand what's happening to us and not suffer without knowing why.

In addition, somatization can work as a shortcut, when the person tries to resolve something in this way that they can't resolve in the light of reality, of coping. When they are ill, they end up withdrawing from that conflictive environment, but the psychological conflict will accompany them wherever they are, even on a paradise beach.

The danger for someone with this condition is that they will go to many doctors' surgeries and undergo a large number of tests and procedures that could put their health at risk. If the doctor doesn't suspect or realize that the reason for the complaints may be emotional, he or she may start various treatments, but without results. This will increase the risk of the patient feeling increasingly ill and without hope of improvement. Of course, he or she will be using a lot of medication, at great expense.

Fortunately, somatization can be reversed with a good psychotherapeutic approach. A clinician with sensitivity and insight will be able to help, without it being necessary to go to a psychologist or psychiatrist.

BALANCE BETWEEN KNOWLEDGE AND BEHAVIOR

The corporate world is full of convictions. Many are mistaken. I've already covered some of them here, such as the one that says that personal problems shouldn't be brought into the professional environment. There is, however, a very correct understanding in human resources departments. It can be summed up like this: "**Technical knowledge gets you hired; behavior gets you fired**." In other words, thanks to training, preparation, experience and *expertise*, a person can get a job; however, because of their behavior, despite their ability, that same person can lose their job.

And that's a major difficulty. How do you gauge the behavioral skills of someone who is about to be hired? Complicated. The best you can do is get some clues - which is already very valuable. Analyzing a CV, intellectual and professional achievements and technical skills is easier because it is largely objective and material. On the other hand, it is more intangible to look at the personality, the way the person deals with their daily work, how they fit into and relate to a team. A good psychological assessment can help, but it will hardly eliminate the chances of problems occurring in day-to-day organizational life. This is because the perception of emotional reactions and the psyche deals with expectations, with potential, and will become more visible with the activity itself.

We mustn't forget that when someone is assessed to join a company, they take every rational precaution not to let their true personality show. It's as if they were wearing a costume and a mask to disguise who they really are. There is a certain theatricality to these selections.

Therefore, this is an issue that must be observed by both sides of an employment contract negotiation. During the process, the prospective employer and the prospective employee must be careful to understand what they want from each other and what they can offer, so that there are no frustrations as a result of biased expectations. However, it is in the workplace, in everyday work, that behavior will really be put to the test. And it's up to the employee in particular to ensure that their manners and procedures match their professional qualities.

It's up to organizations to deal with unexpected and unwanted behavior. I've been called upon countless times in companies to mediate behavioral conflict situations. It's not uncommon to come across arrogant, self-righteous people who don't negotiate, who demand, who don't ask, but who command. What to do with this type of person? In the daily rush, two different reactions are most common: cowardly submission or reckless confrontation. However, prudence, the whole truth when talking about impasses, clarity, objectivity and serenity when dealing with conflicting professional relationships are the reactions we should strive for.

It's like in personal life: you marry someone because you see them in a certain way, but difficulties will arise in the marital routine and you'll have to know how to react. One way or another, the goal must be to get around and overcome the situation, the emotional quarrels, and if the goal is not achieved, then a more drastic attitude, that of breaking up, is in order.

In the lives of couples, there is the possibility of seeking couple psychotherapy. In the institution, the intervention of a professional with experience in detecting and dealing with emotional conflicts, as if they were a supervisor, is the right thing to do. However, it is not part of the corporate culture to seek this kind of help from professionals who have the experience and insight to resolve the emotional conflicts embedded in professional relationships.

In family businesses, the situation is even more serious, because when faced with a difficulty with a manager, the process of approaching them is compromised. Each family member will have his or her own point of view, and the search for a solution can be severely hampered. I've seen fathers, as company president, get angry with their sons who didn't accept their ideas, and the problem was carried into their home. Worse management is when conflicts arise between family members. If there isn't a competent, confident and determined manager, who doesn't tend towards one son or another, the company will become unviable.

Furthermore, if you notice any difficulties in the assessment of the professional to be hired, either you address them or you don't hire them. Another moment will be when, once hired, disputes and setbacks arise. Then the competence and mental health of the CEO will make all the difference in dealing with problems. It's important to be clear in your head that situations in which a subordinate expresses themselves in a rude and inappropriate way may not represent disrespect or an attack on the manager. It will be up to the hierarchically superior professional, if they have good perception, to deal with conflicts without taking offense as if it were something personal. Life is full of confusions and raids, from which those who are not offended by other people's difficulties fare better.

Don't forget that if you reach the top of the functional hierarchy, you'll need to have a good ability to perceive and offer solutions to emotional conflicts, dealing with them without there being winners or losers.

By following these paths, it may be less necessary to fire competent people who can become emotionally unbalanced. Behaviors can change, depending on who accompanies the most troubled. I hope that you, the CEO or manager, are the type who can deal competently with relationships. If not, seek the help of a professional who works with the difficulties of emotional life. Your company will thank you.

DO YOU REALLY LOVE ME?

"Do you love me? Are you sure? Do you really?"

"I need to hear that you love me, so I can calm my heart!"

"You haven't said anything about my new clothes, maybe you don't love me anymore..."

"Today you still haven't told me you love me..."

"You know, I've been waiting all day for you to call and tell me that you love me. But maybe you don't love me the way you used to..."

Who hasn't heard, said or thought phrases like these? Many people feel a pressing need to know that they are loved, to hear flattering and passionate expressions, to have their ego massaged. When they hear "yes", that they are loved, even if it's said weakly, inattentively or out of the blue, they calm down for a while and apparently feel satisfied. Yes, satisfied for hours, but then back to the demands again. Then the cycle starts all over again: another wait for declarations or attitudes that tell each other that there is love in that relationship.

A question arises. Why is it necessary to have this ritual of showing that you love someone? Love can't be hidden, it can't be concealed. And it has countless ways of manifesting itself. So there's no point in anguishing over whether there is true love. All you have to do is open your eyes, your ears and feel it on your skin. All it takes is a good dose of *feeling*.

These questions and expectations of demonstrations of love probably come from what each person reads and perceives in their imagination. I'm suggesting that doubt and insecurity don't necessarily come from external things, but from the internal world, from our unconscious, from our **delusions**, fantasies and phantoms that inhabit our imagination. The more fragile we feel, the more we need tangible proof that we are loved. Our partners aren't our parents and they won't look after us as if we were abandoned children.

Have you heard any of these? "You haven't called me once today and now at night you want to get close, you want to have sex"; "Our love has to be nurtured like a plant, it has to be watered every day"; "Those who love answer WhatsApp messages immediately"; "If you love me, don't go out with your friends to have fun without me". This one is terrible: "Give me proof of your love!"

* * *

We're not talking about infatuation either. Well, infatuation is the initial stage of certain relationships, which ends as quickly as it arises - and it's good that it ends. Infatuation confuses us, blinds us, because we develop idealized feelings towards the other - in other words, we adore someone who is not the person we are with. The person who claims to be in love wants to imprison the other, the object of their passion, taking away their initiative and their desires. It's like imprisonment. The only way for this type of bond to evolve is for passion to be transformed into new bonds, other forms of affection - with intimacy, complicity and freedom. I find it more interesting that no one falls in love with us, but only loves us.

Don't lose sight of the fact that everyone offers what they can in a relationship. Not everyone can translate their feelings for each other into affectionate words. For some people, it's difficult to show affection, give a hug, give flowers, leave affectionate notes or give a pleasant surprise. Individuals carry in their luggage experiences linked to the affectionate, loving, care and attention they received in childhood and throughout their lives. These experiences will or will not help each person's ability to show their affectionate and loving skills in future relationships.

The history of our bonds with parents or caregivers in childhood weighs heavily on our relationships. How much affection, care, attention, praise, touch, etc. we received and experienced at other times in our lives. A child who hasn't felt loved is unlikely to be able to show good feelings as an adult. They tend to be locked up, paralyzed, without initiative - which doesn't mean that they can't love others.

One interesting aspect that we see more in men is that they tend to show their affection in bed; in other words, sex is the channel they use to show their love. For women, on the other hand, this may not be the case, because this act confuses love with sexual desire. Sexual desire is poorer, less elaborate and can also arise for other women with whom one is not intimate or does not love. Popular wisdom says that "a couple's problems are solved in bed". Well, such a couple has little intimacy or capacity for love and affection. When sexual interest wanes, what will keep this couple together?

Others understand that one way of offering their love is by being carers and providers in the relationship. They provide all the financial support, are supportive, attentive, get all kinds of perks, spend on gifts and trips and often also give these benefits to their spouse's family members.

However, I'd like to talk about how difficult it is for some people to perceive the other ways of delivering love. It's more pleasant and easier to receive words and gestures that clearly indicate a posture from someone you love. But what about those who are unable to make this traditional, expected delivery? Those who go out to get medicine at dawn; who help their partner's family with financial resources; who take them to the doctor; who don't sleep at night to look after the children while the other sleeps; who don't withdraw in the face of a serious illness; who continue to desire the other sexually, even though they have lost their breasts or part of their sexual potency; or who always offer a look of complicity, as a masterful way of offering their love.

Insecurity about your partner's love is damaging in many ways. In a nutshell, I'd say that doubting your partner's love can lead to a breakdown in the relationship, creating areas of wear and tear. The relationship deteriorates, becoming boring, even unbearable. Who can bear to live with so many demands? It's a burden to prove every day that you care and have affection for the other person, because love should be felt, perceived by the other person, without the need to prove it.

It's nice to receive flowers from someone you love. A piece of jewelry, however simple, also touches the heart. However, it's also possible to use flowers, jewelry and other gifts to deceive the person who wants to feel loved.

Everything is relative in the world of words and gifts; only what we feel and perceive in relation to others is not relative.

Those who need to hear "I love you" may be taking a risk. They can comfort themselves with any pleasant word, be seduced by a special gift, let themselves be carried away by the speech, without actually knowing if their loved one doesn't also share these same litanies, songs and words of a loving nature with someone else.

Life as a couple, my friends, is not a Hollywood movie or a Globo soap opera. To be loved, perhaps you don't need a wealth of touches, beautiful words or grandiose gestures. With the influence of this misguided view so widespread, a lot is said about people who are incapable of expressing their love, perhaps with great injustice, because it may be that love is there, even if it's not communicated.

* * *

I'd like to invite you to a final reflection. I think everyone agrees that the best thing is to be able to receive love in the conventional way, i.e. said, spoken, shown with flowers, touches, etc. However, the most difficult and demanding thing is to develop the ability to perceive how the other person delivers their love, especially when it's not in the conventional way or how we would like to receive it.

Yes, it is necessary to make this subjective reading of the love offered. The perception and certainty that we are loved is based on a sense of security and good inner self-esteem. If this is lacking, we will be eternal sufferers and will need this transfusion of love into our veins every day. However, insecurity will cause the bleeding to continue, and there is no transfusion that will revitalize a fragile and unhealthy ego.

EMOTION RUN OUR LIVES

You wake up. You go to the bathroom. Look in the mirror. You fix your hair, brush your teeth. Then you have breakfast and go about your day's activities. It's more or less like that for all of us. The routine I've just described follows its normality with other activities, all of which focus on the outside, on what we can see and touch. You look in the mirror, touch your hair, see other people, talk to them, handle objects, you name it. You do it all.

But... **Who are you**? Where do all these actions come from? We know it's your body that does them. But who is behind it? Or rather, what is behind your actions?

I'm talking here about our emotions, our psychological or psychic life, which is inherent, omnipresent and determines the course of our lives. We don't see it, we don't touch it. But it's the one in charge, the one that conditions everything we think, do, say, in short, our entire imagination. Let's understand **emotional life** here as everything that guarantees its existence: psyche, mind, conscious, subconscious and unconscious. The habits we maintain, the food we eat, the people we relate to, the successes and defeats of life, how we feel, how we perceive others, our reactions of joy or sadness, all of this and much more depends on the abstract and impalpable emotional life.

So we need to develop an intimacy with our emotions, become familiar with them. We take care of our bodies, exercise, choose our food, select our clothes... But what about the mind? In general, we don't even realize its existence, its fundamental importance. For a more interesting and enjoyable life, to abandon the art of being unhappy and move towards happiness and well-being, there is no other way: we urgently need to take care of our emotions, our mind, so that we can be more intimate and complicit with this powerful entity.

In relational difficulties, we tend to focus more on the concrete, the tangible, on what we know best. We use our reason, our critical judgment, our intelligence to understand the conflict and how to deal with the clash we will have to fight with ourselves or those around us. That's the way people are, they always take the path they feel best prepared for, the safest.

All of life's confusions, sadness, frustrations, misunderstandings, perplexities, in short, everything that distresses, depresses and even paralyzes us is conditioned by what happens inside us. First of all, we need to realize this.

Of course, external factors in real life also shape and complicate our emotions. But the size and repercussions of real problems will depend on how competently, discerningly and imaginatively we read this harsh reality. It's fashionable to talk about stress and how to deal with it. Here too, each of us will build and give the size of our stress, regardless of external factors.

There is a general tendency to believe that only in extreme cases should we stop to think about what is going on in our heads and perhaps even seek professional help. In other words: we only worry about our minds and emotions when there are signs of madness, a limiting psychiatric illness, withdrawal from social life or serious imbalance.

Not at all! In fact, to think that is crazy, foolhardy, irresponsible of oneself. That said, it's important for people to realize that each individual will have their own response to external problems.

What to do then? There is no form, no manual, no single path to follow and be at peace with your mind, obtaining more or less satisfactory results in all areas of your life. Deciding how to take care of your mind is already part of that care. You may be able, in solitude, through reading and reflection, to find yourself and give a good direction to your emotions.

What's more, you can help yourself through conversations, by exchanging ideas with a more intimate interlocutor, a friend, a partner? With people you trust or even with a professional. The ideal is to do all of this. If you can share your anxieties, your victories and your defeats with the people around you, it will do you a tremendous amount of good and will also encourage the other person to do the same. In time: talk to people who don't position themselves as the owners of the truth and who aren't critical, because they won't get in your way.

In organizations, the presence of some intimacy, perception and interaction with the emotional life of those who manage and interact with many people is even more fundamental. Not enough importance is given to emotional life skills and sensitivity on the part of the directors or CEOs who run companies. Technical knowledge is more important there, which is not a bad thing *per se* - but that's not all that matters.

Another field in which emotional issues are highly relevant, but are given little importance, is soccer. Can anyone answer the question of how much influence mental life has on the performance of players and the outcome of matches? I'd say a lot. Childish expulsions, senseless fouls, simulated fouls, aggression, etc. Everything has to do with individual and group psychology.

The case of the 1998 World Cup in France is exemplary. The night before the final, Ronaldo, the "Phenomenon", had a crisis that shook the entire squad - and Brazil ended up losing the final. The crisis was said to be similar to an epileptic seizure, although this was not confirmed. It was later reported in the media that he suffered strong emotional upheavals, related to his girlfriend and family members who were in Paris, as the players were not allowed to socialize outside the camp. So, having ruled out epilepsy, he was left with a crisis of "nerves". What damage that did to the Brazilian soul...

* * *

I want to differentiate between two paths that can lead to emotional or mental illness. One stems from biochemical alterations that occur in the brain and is linked to neurotransmitters (dopamine, serotonin, noradrenaline, etc.). In these cases, there is often a family history of mental illness, which suggests the presence of genetic alterations. In these patients, the use of medication is very likely to be beneficial. Psychotherapy takes a back seat.

The other path to illness is more closely linked to the real or imagined conflicts we harbor in our psyche. In this case, external aspects are less important to the emergence of psychological suffering. This observation is essential, as we come across people who are sad, down, discouraged, anxious, fearful and who have taken various medications without positive results. Psychotherapy is indicated here, in order to discover the psychic origin of these sufferings. Psychotherapy is the equivalent of rescuing someone who has been buried after an earthquake and bringing them back to life.

For example, one boy developed panic attacks every time he had an argument with his mother. It got worse whenever his mother visited him at home. Here, the difficulty of opposing his mother's bossy ways generated the symptoms. The presence of the symptoms drained him of energy and had the function of not showing his mother how angry and irritable he was. She had to get sick to protect the relationship. Of course, the best thing would have been to say what annoyed him, without attacking his mother.

Another case was that of a lady who was bedridden, depressed and not enjoying the benefits of taking various antidepressants. When I assessed her carefully, I could see the problem: her husband insisted that she work, trying to control her life. She feared opposing her husband; she thought this might lead to separation. Her unconscious way out was to become depressed, to stay in bed, without strength, as if this would take away her partner's drive to collect. When she understood this process in therapy, her symptoms improved and she didn't need to continue taking medication.

Sexual difficulties, both male and female, are generally not due to physical, bodily or hormonal problems. More often than not, the origin was emotional (excluding women's loss of libido or desire during the menopause, due to a drop in female hormones).

In conclusion. It's worth keeping an eye on our emotions, both in the areas of individual performance and collective dynamics (in sports, in companies, in the family, etc.). If you can't succeed and move forward with your own resources, it's worth seeking advice from a professional who knows the ins and outs of the psyche - a psychologist or a psychiatrist. It doesn't make much sense to get an engineer for this task, as was done with the relationship consultant for the Brazilian team in the '98 World Cup. Think about it!

LET LIFE TAKE ME...

"*Let life take me, life takes me...*" This is what one of the most iconic sambas in recent Brazilian music says, sung by Zeca Pagodinho. The verses are good, they make for a pleasant song with a good feel. And there - in music - they should stay. In the real world, there's no such thing as letting life take you! It's cold.

As banal and obvious as it may seem, it's always worth reaffirming: you are the one who has to take charge of your life. And the need to remind ourselves of this fact stems from the fact that it is very common for human beings to believe and wish that we can be saved, coordinated or guided by someone else - or even by the randomness of life. Outsourcing obligations, letting life take us and going belly-up - these are some of our most damaging specialties.

Life is neither fair nor unfair, it just happens and often things happen by chance. So it doesn't make sense to say that such and such a thing couldn't have happened, or that we don't deserve something, or that it's an injustice.

To try to make life less painful and complicated and to reduce bad luck, let's try to pay maximum attention to what we do. Yes, I wrote **attention**! We need to look at the demands of everyday life. Leaving at the right time to get to an appointment. Replying to a message or an e-mail. Pay the bills. Cancel a doctor's appointment or a meeting with a friend if we can't make it. Going for a medical check-up, so as not to be surprised by a serious illness. Having fun. Trying to work on something enjoyable. Being as truthful as possible with people, telling the other person something you don't like. Knowing and respecting your limitations. Take care with alcohol and food. Etc. etc. etc.

In an apparently paradoxical way, at the same time as we don't want to take responsibility for our own lives, we always want to be in control of the lives of others. These behaviors seem to be contradictory, paradoxical - but they're not. Fleeing from self-control doesn't contradict the desire to dominate others, because in both cases the motivation is the same: not paying enough attention to life. In refusing to control my own life, I am irresponsible towards myself; in wanting to control someone else's life, the responsibility is feigned, it is unreal, because the consequences of the decisions weigh on the person being controlled, not on me.

So, while you let life take you, you don't want to answer for yourself. You probably have a father, mother, friend or spouse around you who wants to control you. And vice versa. This forms an unhealthy collusion, which is very foolhardy, because simply giving up responsibility for your own life won't get you out of trouble. There will always be someone on duty who wants to take over your life. Be careful, because generally this person on call won't be very competent to look after their own life, let alone yours. The most you'll get is a sense of relief by outsourcing your decisions. The person who apparently decides for you, however, will feel very important. Sad mistake!

But in addition to this more personal transfer, there are more abstract - and much more irresponsible (if that's possible) - outsourcings. Our projections of responsibility are focused on a number of things. The person isn't doing well in life, so they blame their difficulties on others - their boss, their boyfriend, the weather, their parents, the President of the Republic...

However, when you talk to people who do this, you realize that they don't pay enough attention to their own lives. Without realizing it, they become entangled in forms of escape, such as excessive consumption, debt, eating and sexual compulsions, and so on. What matters is running away from decisions or diverting the focus of tension. Of course, this is unhealthy and will not bring results.

The subject then gets busy with any activity in order to have the feeling that they are taking care of their life. But the emotional, the unconscious, realizes that this is a farce - and will give signs that things are not going well. An unconscious possibility of withdrawing from the care of your daily life is to start feeling some symptom of emotional origin, such as discouragement, nervousness and lack of interest. It's as if the person had an alibi and gave themselves permission to neglect their life.

I'd like to comment on some people's expectations of religions. This is the case with religious individuals who misunderstand the willingness to surrender to God. Trusting in a creator being in whom you believe cannot be confused with not deciding and doing nothing, waiting for a superior providence. If you have a belief, don't stop acting, doing or deliberating. That doesn't stop you from believing that some divine force will help you. Even handing over all your decisions to God is an inadequate demand on him! Or do you think that God has nothing more important to take care of than thinking about the decisions you should make and don't? There's a passage in the Bible that goes something like this: "*Help yourself and I will help you.*" Use your faith to be helped, but don't expect God to do it for you. A common example is when believers don't do their part and say: "I've put the solution in God's hands."

In short, it doesn't matter whether it's your spouse, your parents, the government or your boss who is in charge of your life. Try to change that behavior. Don't let life take you; try to take it wherever you want and wherever you can.

The good - or the bad - thing about all this is that the decision will always be yours, even when you think someone else will decide for you. The mechanisms described here are fertile ground for emotional illness, depression, sadness, irritability, dissatisfaction, anxiety, insomnia and many other symptoms. These mechanisms of seeking and encouraging people to take care of us probably stem from childhood relationships. Many parents, in their eagerness to push their children into life, began to make decisions or do things and tasks for them. They imagined that they would grow up impregnated with the knowledge they received by osmosis. However, this backfires - in other words, these children become shy, fearful and uncreative adults.

Some patients ask me what they should do when faced with a complex situation. I immediately reply: "Sometimes I'm not even sure how I should decide things in *my* life. How can I want to decide for you?" Just to remind you: a psychotherapist's job is not to decide other people's lives, but to help them understand their difficulties so that they can make their own decisions.

INCONVENIENT TRUTHS IN BUSINESS

This text is aimed at those who lead people, manage teams and, especially, own businesses.

Would you be able to sit down with your collaborators, with your company's employees, and give them the floor to openly say what they think about you? The best thing to do would be to have one-to-one conversations, with a time to start and end. In any case, would you have the mind, the capacity or the preparation to listen to them?

What's more, let's say you're a somewhat rare case of a leader who is able to listen to opinions and considerations about himself without getting lost in aggressive self-defense reactions, projecting problems onto others. In that case, apart from listening to the opinions of your subordinates, would you be able to get anything out of it?

Finally, would you be able to listen, "digest", react and achieve positive results from this whole process? Well, if you're that guy, your company must be a success and people must enjoy working there. You must have a lot of mental health to give and sell.

Let's extend our goal. This doesn't just have to happen at work. It could also be at home, between parents and children, sons-in-law and fathers-in-law, students and teachers. Can you imagine a conversation at this level that didn't end in a lot of discussion and even more disagreement? Because at home, among our own people, the make-believe of professional relationships tends to break down and can reveal to us in a truer and more sincere way our real "way of being". Whereas in the company we would hear something about ourselves and stop to take a breath, so as not to react excessively, at home we feel more at ease to say whatever comes to mind - and when we are accused, what comes to mind is defending ourselves and attacking back. Sometimes we don't even really understand the interlocutor's point of view and we're already on the attack.

So I believe that in the professional environment this process can be made easier or more complicated if we consider the head of the manager. In the hierarchy of institutions, one would expect those in higher positions - directors, managers, coordinators - to be more adept at dealing with conflicts. But is this really the case, that managers are more capable of dealing with setbacks and listening to opinions that differ from their own? I realize that most of them don't have this differential. They are leaders who are used to giving orders and expecting results.

Companies often look for managers with great intellectual capacity, tangible knowledge of the area in which they will be working, with post-graduate degrees, MBAs, experience, etc. However, relational capacity, sensitivity, the ability to listen, perceive, interact, digest and articulate are not usually assessed.

The least senior employee (theoretically speaking) should have more space and tolerance to say "stupid things". It would be very productive if those higher up in the hierarchy didn't get offended or irritated by an employee's inappropriate remarks.

The danger arises when a manager finds it difficult to face up to this, because in the end they don't think they need to. They believe that, for the company to produce and generate results, it's enough for their employees to be paid on time, put their heads down and work - "*Those who can command, those who need to obey*", they think.

In fact, this happens a lot in companies, sometimes as a built-in thing, so that it doesn't even seem like there could be a different way of relating. However, you can be sure that a respectful, non-regimented relationship environment can motivate employees in a special way, different from financial rewards. The result, in addition to greater productivity and profitability, will be a group of people who feel good, think it's worth working there and feel respected and valued. However, the difficulty lies in the path to achieving this condition and it starts with the leader himself.

The owner of a business, someone who has the merit of generating wealth and jobs, is someone who wields great power. In emotionally unprepared hands, unable to handle so much power without losing themselves, without it **going to** their **heads**. This condition can be harmful - for the employees, for the business and, ultimately, for the employer himself. Add to this the stresses of everyday life, the great responsibilities that weigh on those who have many bills and taxes to pay, and you have a leader who can succumb to emotional issues.

You therefore need to try to reinvent yourself, open up, offer space and give your employees, your collaborators, a voice. After all, you need them to collaborate with you. It's urgent to listen to what those who make up your valuable human capital think - about everything, including you. You can be sure that everyone will grow from this. The gains for the company are obvious: general well-being, productivity, profits. Employees will feel valued and realize that they are an important part of the business. And they will react to this in their duties.

Of course, these conversations won't come about by chance, because our culture doesn't encourage this level of relationship within institutions. Even at home, there is a tendency for parents not to listen to what their children have to say, especially if they are children and teenagers. Imagine if schools created and encouraged these dialogues between teachers and students in a respectful way. In private schools, I think we would have an ideal environment for these experiences. These ideas of mine may seem utopian, a digression, but I don't think they're out of context. It's worth innovating!

But, of course, listening to employees is not enough. You have to listen, think, understand, digest and - most importantly - give back what you have heard and understood. It's common for bosses to try to give this space in their companies, but immediately after the first stage of the process (i.e. the conversation), they react badly, even thinking about taking revenge on the employee who said something they didn't like. Watch out! The chat is just the beginning. You have to handle the repercussions well. Be sure that, after the conversation, the employee will still be suspicious, fearing the boss's reactions. If the boss knows how to listen and react well, making the most of what's useful and dismissing what doesn't make sense, then everyone will move forward together.

However, when the distance to face-to-face dialogues is too great, an initial possibility is to be able to receive suggestions in writing, even without identifying employees.

In fact, this openness is a two-way street. If employees realize that they can express themselves freely with their bosses, they will be more receptive to demands and charges - as long as they are fair and well-placed, of course. Realize that there is simply no reason not to do this. Imagine that, on top of everything else, you'll have a team willing to take on tasks, to do what's asked of them with dedication, and not just out of the obligation of someone who needs a paycheck at the end of the month. Everyone will be rewarded.

The competence of the listener is not only linked to the fact that they agree with what they hear, but also to their ability to deal with something they don't agree with, which may even be unfair or inappropriate. This is where sensitivity, security and self-confidence come in - in short, the mental health of the manager.

As I write this, I receive a WhatsApp message from the gardener who looks after my family's house on the coast. It said: "*Since you didn't come this weekend, I decided to send you a photo to show you how nice the garden and lawn look.*" In that message, I noticed the care and affection with which the gardener looks after my things. He has always made a good impression on me; I like him. I immediately replied to the message, saying: "I'm glad I found you. I really like you and the way you look after my things." It was good of me to reply, but I confess that it's not an easy thing to do, something that springs up spontaneously within my soul.

It's good to remember that our reactions are more linked to the speed of the emotions we feel than to the process of thinking. Emotion moves at the speed of light, while rational thought moves at the speed of sound, which is slower. Therefore, we tend to react impulsively, through the emotion felt at a given moment, since the word elaborated through thought is less rapid and depends on the damned emotions.

IN SEARCH OF PERFECTION

Many people don't rest until everything they do is just right, just perfect, according to their own criteria. The problem is that, when it comes to perfection, we're like a dog trying to catch its tail. If we don't stop trying, we'll reach exhaustion, physical and mental exhaustion or abandon the task. The perfection I'm describing here is in relation to something unattainable, because it doesn't refer to the task to be done, but to the internal dissatisfaction of the person doing it. There is a dissociation, a disconnection between the work to be done and the desire of the person doing it. It's as if I asked the perfectionist to clean a suit of clothes, and he tore it up from washing it so much; or he didn't even get around to cleaning it, because he'd be ruminating on what cleaning product to use and so wouldn't be able to start the job.

I don't mean that always trying to do the best, constantly striving for the best, is a bad thing. Not at all! Having your peers recognize the success of your work is very comforting. Perfectionists don't really know where they want to go, because they have no tolerance for what is possible, so they end up aiming for the impractical. Many simply become paralyzed. I've seen people who, not being able to do what they think is best, simply couldn't get out of their seats on a task because, unconsciously, in their minds the opposite of perfection is mediocrity.

This book might not make it out of the drawer if it were in the home of a perfectionist. There is always room for improvement, there are always better words, better ways of saying what we want to convey. A piece of writing will never be as finished as its author would like, but you have to play with reality and put an end to it.

Also, the series of videos "**5 minutes with psychiatrist Nelio Tombini**",* which I've been recording about relational life, wouldn't have come to fruition.

---

* https://www.youtube.com/user/Psicobreve

During the first recordings, I was very insecure, I wanted to repeat the recordings, I watched the videos and I didn't like them. The cameraman helped me; when I watched the videos and didn't like them, he said that they were good, that he had experience of recording other people and that I communicated well. I believed him! We agreed that the videos would not be edited, that they would be posted without us redoing anything, except in the event of a gross error. If I had perfectionist tendencies, the cameraman would have abandoned me or charged me a lot more for the time I spent making a video.

In these cases and in most situations, there is no reason to cling to endless and insane corrections. Not least because - if you're prone to perfectionism - usually no one other than the perfectionist notices the corrections. In other words, more often than not, all the work these people put in is not noticed by anyone, and even the perfectionist will doubt whether it was worth changing so much.

For these and other reasons, the perfectionist is a great sufferer, despite the fact that he thinks he is very important. As he thinks his works and actions must be perfect, he is always demanding of himself - and thinking that he is under constant scrutiny from others. Realize how big this ego is! He believes he is the center of attention, his own and someone else's, so he can never afford to make a mistake.

For all these reasons, the perfectionist will be someone who is very disciplined, very careful with everything - and therefore very worried and anxious. However, life goes beyond our control and so do people. The desire for control is part of the possibilities for understanding the intricacies of the perfectionist's imagination. They want everything to be according to their will and their thinking. In this way, the search for refinement can unconsciously reveal a subterfuge for not doing the task.

If the person was healthier, they would say they wouldn't do the task, but if they were more troubled and confused by their emotions, they might cling to the pursuit of perfection, which would lead them to not do the task. Think about it! Human beings are not logical at all! And perfectionists are people who are very good at thinking and arguing, but have little desire or ability to listen.

Excessive discipline, demands and combinations are part of their personality. If you arrange something, like a timetable, being five minutes late can be felt by them as a great disregard. They won't tolerate a used cup not being washed immediately. An unopened tube of toothpaste can be grounds for separation. For him, life has only one path; and the truth is the one that is seen through his magnifying glass.

We can consider other feelings that these people develop about themselves. It's very likely that they hide insecurities in the cellars of their emotions, ideas that they won't be valued and that nothing they do will be admired by others. They don't deliver what they should and this attitude tends to arouse frustration, irritation and discontent in others, rather than admiration. This creates an endless vicious circle - unless you seek the intervention and help of a psychotherapist. Medication won't help to break this cycle, except to reduce anxiety about the way you act.

It's hard to get a compliment from these people. They work with a telescope to find other people's faults - and they'll always point out what's missing, even if 99% of it is good. You could say that they are castrators of your abilities and achievements. Relationships with them will also be complicated, because those around them get tired of their demands. The result: they move away or fight. It is impossible for a perfectionist to be creative, because creativity involves a certain permissiveness to think, experiment, change, make mistakes and do things differently from the conventional. In their emotional life, they will find it difficult to show their affection. They tend to be less affectionate and loving. They are more objective and pragmatic when it comes to relationships.

* * *

At certain times, in very specific and repetitive tasks, this behavior may fit in and give positive results. I'm talking about services such as flight controllers, pilots, security technicians, employees who handle the sterilization of materials, in other words, jobs where it is necessary to adhere to strict protocols, with high technical standards and impeccable quality.

* * *

It's important to note that people with obsessive disorders are perfectionists. In these cases, they may have other symptoms associated with obsessive-compulsive rituals.

WHY ARE WE SO INTOLERANT?

Open the newspaper and read all the headlines. Turn on the radio and TV. You're sure to find a fair amount of news involving intolerance. Especially in the politics and police sections. It happens in traffic, in schools, in parks, in soccer, in relation to sexual identity, between neighbors and even within homes. There are many cases of fights, arguments, disagreements and even deaths that result from a lack of dialog, from people's inability to tolerate each other and to tolerate adverse situations that displease them.

This text comes from an interview I gave on Jornal do Almoço (RBS TV, Porto Alegre), about intolerance. It was in March 2016, but I could give this interview any day, because there are similar cases in all of them. And this is simply because we are, by nature, grumpy, irritable and demanding beings. To begin with, human beings are uncompromising with themselves, they demand too much of themselves, they are always demanding themselves, blaming themselves, which ends up causing a state of constant anxiety.

However, we repeat this pattern at home, at work and even during leisure time with friends. My soccer team is the best and I can even get involved in bar fights for it. My political party is the most decent and I'll defend it on the streets, even fighting with relatives. Some people think that their religion is the only one that makes sense; the others would be enemies. And so on. Social networks enter our privacy, our rest and our homes all the time, sowing intrigue and potentially wreaking havoc on our emotions.

Intolerance is closely linked to the way we think and understand what goes on inside and outside of us. The starting point for all this is beliefs. We are driven and guided by conceptions, prejudices, pre-judgments, in other words, by preconceived ideas rooted in our imagination. Faced with a fact, a disagreement, an attitude, a word, we can react more on impulse than by thinking about what we are seeing and feeling. Intransigence is directly related to how we read what has happened, how we interpret it and how we feel about it - and not necessarily to what happened or the fact itself. In other words, the interpretation of the fact is worth more than the fact itself. Amazing, isn't it?

Let's not ignore the fact that it's very difficult, in a moment of tension, irritation or anxiety, to search our minds for a healthier and more refined resource before taking an intemperate action. If we think we are omnipotent, in the sense that we can do anything, the risk of being inflexible increases. The grandiose person, who thinks they are more than others, will also have strong tendencies towards intolerance.

Notice that in these last two paragraphs I'm looking more at intrinsic or unconscious aspects of people, and not at what's going on outside, in the external world. Right! We need this subjectivity or reflection to better understand the workings of individuals who behave as the masters of reason and truth.

This condition has been exacerbated by what we have experienced in Brazil in recent years. The population, in general, is very disbelieving, because it has found itself helpless and betrayed in various ways by those to whom it entrusts its care. In other words, our representatives in public administration, in the courts and in parliament are systematically failing to do what they were appointed to do, and are instead making the most of their positions at any and all costs. In times of the internet and a more dynamic press, we follow these movements in real time.

* * *

Perhaps the great broth of culture that has generated and nourished the souls of intolerant people began within their own families. Parents who are truculent, abusive, violent, who generate a feeling of emptiness and dejection in their children. Situations of great deprivation in childhood. These harmful experiences can be the basis of these intransigent individuals. It's as if, in the face of any experience in which they feel mistreated, repressed feelings from their childhood experiences come to the surface.

Therefore, our intolerance can increase in proportion to our anger. The problem is that we always tend to look for people to blame for our justified dissatisfaction. Nowadays, we have a large number of real characters to pin our frustrations on. So, when we're in the queue at the supermarket and the person in front is late, when we feel disrespected in traffic, when a family member says something we don't like, all our pent-up indignation comes to the surface. Of course, at that moment we don't remember what's behind the outburst of rabid intolerance.

The intolerant person par excellence is still a little dictator, in the sense that he doesn't respect the right to the opinion of others, when he attacks someone who acts or thinks in a way he doesn't agree with. In short, this *little life* is complicated and difficult, but let's get on with it, because we need to live it.

* * *

To combat all this, the formula is very simple - and can be summed up in one verb: **think**. It is this ability that distinguishes us from each other. How does everyone build up their ability to think? Of course, we react to various everyday situations. Before the actual reaction, we feel, we perceive, and these stimuli should pass through reason, which is thinking. The problem is that we often react and then think. That's how many humans are. You have to reflect, always policing yourself, controlling yourself. If you want to be intolerant of something, let it be your own intolerance. Thoughts can escape our control, but actions cannot. These can be shaped by our character, our perceptions and the constant attention we pay to the impulses that arise within.

Please don't forget that when we drink or use other drugs, intolerance will certainly multiply 100-fold and we will lose the ability to deal with it; in other words, it will crush our reason, thinking, intelligence, culture, religiosity, etc. When I say drinking, it's not necessary to drink your fill. A few pints of beer or a shot of spirits can change our ability to perceive and react.

In short, intolerance is part of the human imagination. There's no way that we can't have some degree of this bitterness. The extent to which we act intolerantly towards the facts of life will depend on our emotional or unconscious state, how healthy or unhealthy it is. The intolerant person gets bored and can fight with the world, because they are very rigid, demanding and uncompromising with themselves. In this way, they try to get rid of their anxieties by putting them out there, unloading them on others; however, this will not bring results, because everything comes back to the subject.

In short, intolerance develops and is built up more in our internal, emotional or psychic world. The event that generates the intolerance will serve as a trigger, generating reactions that are often unintentional. Often, after the traumatic episode, the person rethinks and is not happy with their attitude.

IS LIFE TREATING YOU BADLY?

One day, I was talking to a distressed friend. His wife didn't want to stay married. She spoke in a sad way, like someone who is very discouraged. Of course, separations are always painful, even for those who take the initiative. Some can be very traumatic. I listened to his annoyances, sadness, indignation and irritation.

But what struck me most was the feeling that he was being wronged. Throughout his lengthy account, this was the most emphasized note. He said that, in 15 years of marriage, he had given so much of himself to his wife that he simply couldn't understand why she no longer wanted to live with him. He thought that, after such dedication, only a very unjust and ungrateful person would think of leaving him.

"I've always done everything for her. I helped her to study, giving her intellectual and financial support. I took her wherever she wanted to go. I talked to her, listened to her, cared for her, in short, I did everything I could. I paid her bills. When she went out with her friends, I also made myself available for transportation." These were more or less the terms used.

I could see in his story that he used a subliminal and unconscious strategy in his marriage, apparently loving, to control his wife's movements. It was as if his partner was handcuffed to him. In fact, he tried to control her life, disguising it with the cloak of love. This attitude gave the woman a sense of fragility; in other words, she could never think of living without his protection. Of course, everything was done in the quiet of his imagination, to ensure that he would never be abandoned by his apparently submissive, fragile and dependent wife. However, as we already know, his ploys didn't work...

After a lot of talking, a lot of arguing in favor of his qualities, saying (in other words) that it wasn't fair for his wife to abandon him, he looked at me with a questioning face. He obviously expected me to agree. He probably thought that friends "are there to support you in any situation", so that I should be on the side of the apparently wronged party.

I thought about it and answered as truthfully as I could, asking questions that I answered myself, more or less along these lines:

- Why did you make so many sacrifices for your wife? Why did you give so much of yourself? You didn't do any of this out of obligation - or necessity! You freely and consciously chose to dedicate yourself to that woman! You certainly had your reasons! According to your account, you liked her, you had affections and loves and a pleasurable sex life. Didn't she love you in the past? I bet she did! Didn't she respond to your feelings? I bet she did! Didn't she make concessions and efforts to make the relationship enjoyable? I bet she did!

Of course, the subject had been discussed by the couple. His wife didn't wake up overnight with the idea of separation in her head! She had been showing signs of drifting apart, both affectively and sexually, but he denied it, imagining that it would pass. The final point was when she said she would like to go on a trip with a work colleague, logically without him being present.

I told all this to my friend, who was following my train of thought and, although a little dismayed by my words, apparently digesting my ideas. The couple's relationship had reached a point where one side simply didn't want it anymore. There was no betrayal, no deceit, nothing like that. I asked him:

- And then, the moment she wants out of the relationship, you allow yourself to present the bill, the invoice for your dedication to her, putting her in the ungrateful role?

* * *

Another situation, very similar to the previous one. However, here the interlocutor was not in the position of the one who is "abandoned", but in the position of the one who "abandons". After years of marriage, he decided to leave home. So he was under intense pressure from his partner. It was something like: *"After all these years of love and dedication, will you leave me?"* In fact, his wife's stance was beginning to have an effect. This friend invited me for coffee and a chat, because he felt guilty and wanted to share his anxieties with me. He was seeing himself as a traitor, an ingrate.

The woman said she didn't deserve to be abandoned because for years she had done everything for him, including giving up her studies and work to "take care of him". Seeing that he was falling for it, I asked him: "Did you ever force her to do any of those things?" The answer was: "Never."

Why do so many people act like this lady? How I'd love to hear from her and find out why she's leading her life in this way... I would like to reflect on how these people's unconscious mind works.

The choice to do more for others than for oneself must have some unnoticed motivation in the imagination. I think that when someone invests more of their energy in looking after others than themselves, it's because they don't think it's worth it or they don't have the desire to invest in their own life. This type of person unconsciously chooses a loved one, a spouse, a child, a collaborator, in short, to turn into their reason for living and thus turns their back on their own life. Also striking is the desire to control the other, which gives a feeling of power. The one who is apparently subjected also plays the role of controller, but in the opposite way.

It's as if the controller built a wall to imprison the person being cared for. However, this wall may collapse, causing the prisoner to escape. This is when the jailer realizes that he too was inside the fortress; however, he thinks he won't know how to live outside of it.

I'm not disdaining marriage and I don't applaud break-ups *a priori*. I know the suffering that occurs on these occasions. What I want to share here is this attitude of the supposedly wronged party, who tries to turn a loving relationship into a contract, in which one party has done more and should be rewarded. Now, a relationship should be governed by affection and love; emotional blackmail and undue and unreasonable demands cannot be part of it.

* * *

These examples serve to illustrate a hard truth: life as it is, "life as it is" (as Nelson Rodrigues would say). We are responsible for our actions and our choices. There is practically no situation in which we are not responsible - directly or vicariously - for something that happens to us or is done to us, even when that dear person has disappointed you bitterly. Think about it. This disappointment probably has more to do with an exaggerated expectation that you yourself created than with a fault on the part of the person, the object of your projection.

We tend to believe that our sufferings and our devotions oblige our relatives and friends and the whole universe to throw confetti at us, pay homage to us and pay tribute to us. Not at all! Often, however, we suffer in silence. That friend to whom we offered a shoulder in times of trouble now doesn't return the gift; the woman who was given a generous gift offers nothing more than a souvenir... Oh, how unfair!

This was the feeling of a couple who once came to see me. From humble beginnings, they had worked hard to give their children an education and the best possible life. Fortunately, one of their children succeeded in life. After graduating, he got a good job, got married and started to enjoy life, including traveling with his wife. After the first trip, in which the young man went out into the world to take advantage of the status he had achieved, his parents began to show strong resentment.

At first, they said it without saying it; then they began to explicitly declare to their son the feeling of injustice that affected them. *"How could he go out into the world having fun and being happy, accompanied by his wife, while we, after a lifetime of sacrifices, would stay at home and grow old?"* Well, the boy hadn't abandoned his parents; he was just living his life.

Could he, in addition to the financial help and attention he already gave his parents, take them on a trip together? Perhaps so, but there was nothing obliging him to do so, so demanding it was an exaggeration. We could imagine that his parents' dedication to their son wasn't for a loving reason, but for something very pragmatic. As if it were an investment, to be paid back in the future.

How many times have we heard someone say: *"So-and-so screwed me over, passed me over"*? The reality is usually different. I hope you won't be upset by what I'm saying here. The fact is that we facilitate or create the right conditions for being screwed over. I'll give you my own testimony. Whenever I've been tricked or screwed over, there has been active or passive participation on my part. When I realize that I've helped to get screwed over, I get upset, but I also calm down, because there's no point in getting angry at the offender.

If we believe that we have been cheated, passed over, wronged, life will always owe us - a debt that will never be repaid. Resentment and complaining will then turn into psychiatric symptoms such as depression, sadness, anxiety, insomnia, irritability and aggression. The person will feel ill, but there will be no remedy to get them out of this malaise.

* * *

In all the cases I've presented here, and in countless others, the problem is always the same: people with a disproportionate feeling of injustice, of being owed money and everything else - the world, life, people owe them attention, rewards and justice. Life isn't like that.

We can also get sick and think we didn't deserve it, because we've always been good, charitable, loyal, ethical, etc. Well, life takes its course, regardless of what we think or expect of it. For people who haven't had the capacity or the mind to take good care of their lives, you have to tell the truth: **life doesn't owe you anything**.

KNOW THYSELF

It is necessary, it is recommended for your life and your psychological health that you become more intimate with yourself. How? By developing your emotional side, contemplating your inner issues and sharpening your own perceptions of what you might call your soul, your emotional or unconscious self. You need to know that there is a "little world" inside each of us, which can help or hinder our daily lives, and which is usually very secret. Those who develop these skills will also be better able to perceive the subjectivity and subliminal messages of relationships in general.

It's common for people to seek professional development and success, to become what we call successful. And what are the main paths to this, to success and relevance among the communities we want to be recognized by?

One possibility is to be competent to do business and earn a lot of money. Another path is the intellectual, cognitive path, which depends on our intelligence, how much we study, how much we read and how much we dedicate ourselves to growing intellectually. In this way, we acquire and demonstrate ownership and authority on the topics that interest us; we have something to say or do about these issues and then we will be recognized by society. We will also be able to receive good pay and the much-desired financial gain. The world will look at you and see what you have, where you are, what you have achieved.

The other path is somewhat more tortuous, less easy - but with more consistent results that can make our lives more meaningful. I'm talking about the nuances of emotional life. This is how we can differentiate ourselves from the point of view of having more inner consistency and perceiving ourselves as having better mental health. Development and intimacy with emotional life are not as accessible as intellectual and financial development.

If we want to know more about the nuances of our mind, we will find ourselves with fewer resources available to us, because we may need interlocutors who can open the floodgates of our unconscious. We don't learn this at school, in books, in the media or in mental health programs offered by public bodies.

Well, the idea of writing this book comes precisely from the desire to transfer a little intimacy, knowledge, skills and tools to deal better with our emotions. Other ways to follow this path are poetry, literature, reading and psychotherapy; or even sharing perceptions with a good friend who has sensitivity and insight into emotional life.

Both cognitive (or intellectual) and emotional intelligence are important for all of us. However, the latter is more relevant to the comfort and serenity of our soul. If we don't have it well resolved, there's no point in developing various skills, because we won't know how to use them or we won't get the best out of them. No amount of knowledge and no material achievement can make emotional suffering go away. However, this is what can give meaning to everything, to earning money, having power... That way, you can feel good and enjoy the life you've achieved.

For example, when faced with a loss or bereavement, suggesting that the bereaved travel abroad or use their financial resources to buy interesting goods will not relieve their pain. What can overcome this suffering is the capacity for introspection, reflection and intimacy with oneself and one's peers.

Understanding all of this makes a big difference in our daily lives, both in the biggest tasks and challenges and in the simplest ones. If I'm clear with myself about my limitations and capabilities, I won't be shaken if someone tries to take out their frustrations on me. A bad-tempered boss can try to undermine the peace of a good employee by being strict with them or blaming them for something they didn't do. However, if this employee is more intimate with his or her emotional life, he or she will be able to see how his or her boss is getting in the way and trying to put a rancor on him or her that doesn't make sense and should be the boss's own fault. This perception helps them not to be put down by someone else's craziness. This example applies to parents, children and spouses who try to pin their anxieties and frustrations on those around them.

Then you'll say: *"But what about my dignity, my modesty, my esteem in the face of these abuses?"*

Well, well! This has nothing to do with esteem. If you realize that it's the other person's problem and not yours, your dignity won't be scratched! If you realize that the other person is trying to pin something on you that doesn't belong to them, you'll be less likely to get stressed. You'll then be able to address the issue without getting nervous and showing your perception of what's going on.

A personal example: traffic. Traffic can bring me conflict and unhappiness. It can irritate me, make me lose my temper, make me feel uncontrollably angry. Or not! Faced with the emotions described above, I quickly try to collect my thoughts and abort some risky action. How do I do that? I think that I've done things similar to the one that's upsetting me - and I also imagine that the reckless person didn't take that action against me directly. Therefore, I have nothing to do with it. Thinking like this, in a way that actually corresponds to the facts, usually calms me down, because I don't let myself be contaminated by other people's bad feelings.

Sexual performance - or libido - is very sensitive to any psychological unrest. If we are in the slightest bit upset with our partner or with ourselves, the chances of this having a negative impact on our sexual performance are extremely high. A man can take Viagra, but he may not get an erection, because the problem is not in his penis, but in his **head**.

We are susceptible to unexpected and unknown emotional discomfort. There is always some degree of anxiety, apathy, sadness, irritability, sleepless nights, etc., all without it being characterized as a psychiatric illness. We tend to want to get rid of these experiences as quickly as possible. What are the most common and most inappropriate ways to get rid of these feelings? Drinking or taking a black-band tranquilizer (Rivotril). However, those who are more intimate with themselves won't need to use these devices, as they will seek the answers to these anxieties within themselves. That's the whole point of being intimate with yourself.

I remember a situation that happened with a psychotherapy group I ran at Santa Casa in Porto Alegre, with SUS patients. Before the session began, the patients stood in a small queue to renew their prescriptions for the medication they were using. One day, a girl decided to skip the queue. I promptly told her to wait at the end of the queue and that she would be seen soon. She went to the back of the queue and, as she positioned herself in the last seat, she fainted. She fell to the floor, but without hurting herself. There was a rush of concern from the other patients, but I calmed them down by saying: "Don't worry, she'll soon wake up and get up!" Of course, I knew a little about her psychic functioning. She was very spoiled by her father, to the point where they sat in the group holding hands, as if she were a helpless little child. After a few minutes, she got up and stayed in line.

Afterwards, we talked in group therapy about what had happened and what the fainting meant. She was clearly irritated with me for not treating her like my beloved little daughter, not giving her preference over the other patients. When she fainted, she unconsciously wanted me to go and help her and stop paying attention to the others. After this meeting, and with the therapeutic intervention of the group, this girl was able to control her desires and, in the face of frustration, use other healthier resources than fainting. This is yet another example of how intimacy with our feelings, with our emotions, will do our lives a lot of good.

If we have this intimacy, we'll certainly be better equipped to lead a less psychologically painful life and be able to go against the **art of being unha-ppy**. Think about it.

ATTENTION DEFICIT HYPERACTIVITY DISORDER

Attention deficit hyperactivity disorder (ADHD) is a recurring concern among parents of school-age children and young people and among my audience on Facebook and YouTube. It's a diagnosis made with increasing frequency among children and even adults, in Brazil and around the world.

Unlike other medical specialties, psychiatry does not rely on precise tests to make diagnoses. The use of X-rays, magnetic resonance imaging, brain scans, blood tests, scintigraphy and electroencephalograms are not helpful in making psychiatric diagnoses. Our diagnoses are basically made by talking to patients and their families.

Notice the name given to this syndrome: **attention deficit hyperactivity** disorder. The child's inability to study, concentrate and complete tasks must be associated with hyperactivity, as well as restlessness, motor agitation, lack of whereabouts and physical restlessness. Parents and teachers need to be informed when a child has this condition. They don't sit still in class, talk non-stop, get in the way of their classmates, don't listen to instructions, etc. At home it's no different: they are agitated and find it difficult to listen to instructions and complete tasks.

What I see these days are patients complaining of a lack of concentration and problems with attention and memory, both in children and adults. Who doesn't realize at some point that they're lacking concentration? Our social and working environment encourages poor attention and concentration, as we are bombarded with various demands. We're reading, looking at WhatsApp, watching a game on TV and talking to a friend, all at the same time. It's difficult to maintain a high level of concentration on so many tasks. What we often see are people who are calm and inattentive.

We've seen a big jump in the number of children, in Brazil and in the Western world, diagnosed and taking medication for ADHD. There are psychiatrists, both here and in the United States, questioning and criticizing what they say is an excess of diagnoses. The problem is that, in the wake of a misdiagnosis, psychostimulant medication is prescribed - the best known being Ritalin.

The big question to consider is the extent to which the symptoms presented by children may be the result of psychological or emotional maladjustments, originating in family conflicts, usually between the parents. Children are very perceptive of feelings, confusion and emotional disorders within the family. Many parents argue, treat each other badly, are rude and imagine that if they don't fight in front of the child, he or she won't notice the family's maladjustments. That's a mistake. Being a child doesn't mean being an idiot or mentally retarded.

Children are more perceptive than adults when it comes to their emotional life. In many cases, children show a certain dejection, disinterest, apathy and, consequently, a lack of attention - not because they have a mental illness, but because they feel the atmosphere at home is heavy. It's not uncommon to see children who are agitated, scattered and irritable, displaying everything that someone with attention deficit hyperactivity disorder has. The cause could possibly be emotional.

Children's imaginations are robust, creative and perceptive. They are able to imagine that their parents are fighting because they are not behaving well, for example. In this way, they feel guilty for the couple's quarrels. In addition, the child's emotional illness may be an unconscious way of attracting the family's concern to themselves, taking them away from their parents' quarrels. It would almost be a magic solution. It's as if it saves the marriage - "Now they'll be upset with me, not with each other".

The child becomes psychologically ill. They may be afraid to sleep alone, urinate in bed again, be afraid to go to school, become agitated and lack concentration. In this way, the focus of concern shifts to the child and no longer to the parents' conflict. However, this will not resolve the conflicts of the elders; on the contrary, it could further destabilize the already fragile family.

This will give the impression that the child has an attention deficit and is hyperactive, when in fact they are just reacting to their environment. In fact, they act like a sentinel, sending out signals when danger is approaching. If there are serious and constant family conflicts, the child will be the first to show signs - through school, eating and sleeping disorders, which are representatives of their emotional conflicts.

It can be a relief for parents to all go to a child psychiatrist and come away with a diagnosis, medication and the idea that the problems will be solved objectively. It would be more complicated and embarrassing if this professional said that the child was troubled by family conflicts. In that case, the real treatment would be with the parents, in psychotherapy, and not with the child as an isolated target for treatment.

We must also consider the shortage of psychologists and psychiatrists with adequate skills and training to assess and carry out psychotherapy on children. These difficulties are great in the SUS and in health insurance plans. So, without the *expertise* to take the right approach, we resort to simplification: medication. Another relevant aspect relates to the socialization of medicine. Health insurance plans pay low prices for psychiatric consultations and even less for psychotherapy, which encourages quick appointments and the use of medication. Psychotherapies are more laborious and require more time to assess and monitor the patient.

The main treatment should be for the family, the focus of the conflicts, not just the child. A hasty misdiagnosis, which only looks at the effects, can lead to a lack of understanding that the child has ADHD. That's why it's essential to pay attention primarily to the causes, understanding what's behind the agitation and concentration difficulties.

It is important to diagnose ADHD. It stems from biochemical problems linked to the functioning of the brain; in other words, it is an organic or physical disease. Identifying and treating ADHD in children will prevent a series of other problems, a chain of inadequacies and disquiet in adult life.

We know that if ADHD is not managed properly with medication, it can lead to learning difficulties for the child and disturbances in relationships with their peers. If left untreated, this disorder can turn into other illnesses in adolescence and adulthood. There are clear criteria for increased drug use, impulsivity and mood disorders. It is estimated that 40% of adults will have symptoms of the disorder if they were not treated in childhood. Adults have similar symptoms to children, but less intense. They can also show ups and downs in mood, short temper, impulsiveness and disorganization.

To reassure readers, I have to say that a well-trained child psychiatrist will be able to distinguish between a child's emotional problems that just look like ADHD and the neurological and biochemical disease itself. Another interesting fact is that when in doubt about the diagnosis, psychiatrists can carry out a therapeutic test, using medication for a few weeks. In this way, the diagnosis can be clearer and more effective, resulting in the symptoms improving or not.

SUBTLE MENTAL ILLNESS

When we talk about mental illness, we immediately think of serious situations such as madness or psychosis, bipolar disorder, severe depression, drug addiction or panic disorder. These diagnoses are better known and more impactful. They cause suffering and significant obstacles in patients' lives. These are cases in which there is a clear limitation, a permanent suffering that causes patients and their families to seek help.

But there are also other, more subtle, more nebulous psychological problems, from which many people may suffer, but without clearly realizing the source of the problem. As absurd as it may seem at first glance, the fact is that virtually no one is immune to some kind of emotional suffering, whether temporary or persistent.

In each of us there is an inner, unconscious and permanent struggle between desires and the repressions against them, generating what we call psychic conflicts. As well as internal repression, we also have culture, morals and laws that try to stifle these desires.

These desires can be linked to things that are not acceptable in social life. Cheating, lying, stealing, having inconvenient sexual fantasies, not fulfilling promised tasks, wanting to hit someone, feeling angry, not paying a debt, wanting to kill an enemy. Dreams also represent repressed unconscious desires. In this constant and incessant struggle, many of the symptoms that shake the mind arise.

Psychic conflicts are transformed and appear in our daily lives through many symptoms - anxieties, fears, depression, anger, irritation, insomnia, somatization, obsessions, apathy, learning difficulties and sexual problems.

Did you realize the potential of our unconscious to cause us problems? So the question arises: **How can laypeople clearly attest to the presence**

of the unconscious? Answer: pay attention to dreams, acts of failure and symptoms of psychic origin.

In dreams, there are often strong anxieties or experiences of imminent disasters and deaths, which can wake us up in the dead of night. Dreams are sensations and experiences that have no basis in fact. They appear disguised, segmented, timeless and incomprehensible. We shouldn't be frightened by them, even when they bring a lot of suffering (like nightmares). Bad dreams are not a sign of danger or bad omens. You can dream of a black cat, death and disasters and life will continue without risk. Unless, after the dream, you get careless or do something silly.

I will repeat several times in this book that psychiatry is a specialty of medicine that walks in the dark, because we don't have tests to help us make an accurate diagnosis. Understanding what causes emotional suffering will depend on the professional's competence when assessing the patient or talking to family members. Because of this subjectivity, we may have different diagnoses and understandings of the same patient from one psychotherapist or psychiatrist to another.

To help you understand how our unconscious or imaginary mind can create traps for us, I'll tell you about a few situations.

* * *

A young man was competent in his academic life, professional career, friendships and love relationships. Suddenly, however, he began to lose interest in his activities and withdrew from people and work. He had gone to a psychiatrist and started taking medication, but without results.

He reported that he began to feel strange after his father left home, with whom he had a very bad relationship. The father went on to live with another woman; the mother was very unhappy with the separation and became depressed, spending a lot of time in bed, crying and blaming the father for the poor quality of her life. The woman blamed all her unhappiness on her ex-husband, as if she were an invalid or an abandoned child.

Being unwell in bed reinforced the idea that someone had to look after her. Her son, who also saw his father as the culprit, felt responsible for rehabilitating his mother. What happened? He began to lose the ability to take care of his own life. He also became depressed and lacked energy. So he allowed himself to stay close to his mother, who felt better with her son by her side.

It's clear that the boy could and should support his mother, but without ever neglecting himself. As he became aware of the construction of this subtle or unconscious illness, he began to work on building a different relationship with his mother and also with his father. He realized that the separation was no catastrophe, just an accident with no victims.

Another situation occurred on a flight. When the passenger sitting next to me heard that I was a psychiatrist, he told me the story of a friend who could no longer do his job. This friend decided to work for himself, but his wife was against the plan because she wanted the security of a salary at the end of the month. The couple had a few arguments and the friend gave in to his wife's wishes. He continued in the same job, but began to show signs of panic when he arrived at his workplace. He started taking medication, but he was still unwell.

I told my armchair neighbor that the problem to be treated was not panic, but conflict with his wife. In order not to go against his wife, the man submitted and, in return, his imagination picked up the bill, developing symptoms of panic. There's no pill that can solve that! See how easy it is to stumble under the influence of the emotional, psychological side.

* * *

I call the two situations I've just described **subtle mental illness**, since they were constructed in the imagination of their protagonists without them realizing it. The boy in the first case had to fall ill in order to try to take care of his mother. As he realized and incorporated this new view of his dejection and apathy, he began to improve his life. With his improvement, he also helped his mother resolve her seemingly endless grief. The husband in the second event had conflicts with his wife and not with his work, as it might seem.

Notice how difficult it is to understand the human mind and the pitfalls it creates for all of us. In these cases, psychotherapy can help to unravel ingenious and almost inextricable traps.

Today there is a tendency to medicate people without caution and without criteria. In the vast majority of cases, it's not even psychiatrists who prescribe, but other doctors, such as clinicians, gynecologists, neurologists and other specialists. Medicines have been very helpful in improving psychiatric illnesses. When suffering is based on existential or emotional problems, medication helps little or not at all. On the contrary, as they are not properly indicated, the symptoms will remain and the patient may be left with the idea that their problem has no cure.

For subtle mental illnesses, there is nothing better, more efficient and more effective than understanding and treating the emotional background - in this case, through psychotherapy.

ADVERTISING ABUSES

A few years ago, there was an advertising campaign for an underwear brand on TV and in the media, starring a famous model. The model stars in the scenes, in which she talks to her husband, who doesn't appear in the images.

There are three scenarios:

In the first, the woman informs us that she has overdrawn her husband's credit card and her own.

In the second, she tells them that her mother will be moving in with them.

On the third, he says he crashed his car.

The emphasis of the commercial - and the reason for the controversy - is that there are two ways for a woman to talk to her husband: the ***wrong*** way, dressed in conventional clothes, and the ***right*** way, in *sexy* underwear. There was an outcry from many women who felt belittled by the commercial.

I don't want to play the role of the annoying person who sees things where others don't, but I would like to highlight subliminal aspects of the commercial that I believe are abusive to the good health of marital relationships.

First of all, it's clear that the advertisement shows a wife who is averse to dialog, who pushes situations that have already been consummated down her husband's throat. The scenes show a stereotype of a woman who is apparently cool, but who is imposing and disrespectful towards her husband.

Let's see. In the first commercial, she doesn't take proper care of her money. She spends uncontrollably and tells her husband to take care of her excessive spending. In the second, she decides that her mother will move in with the couple, without having talked to her partner. Yet another attitude of disregard for her partner. In the third, well, anyone can crash the car - it wouldn't be necessary to dress up in your underwear for that announcement.

The commercial suggests that sexual seduction produces results and is a good path for women to follow when facing difficulties in their marital relationship. In our culture, the female body is overvalued, to the detriment of a woman's intellect, culture, affections and way of thinking. I remember a saying that disqualifies dialogue in favor of sex: "A couple's problems are solved in bed."

It's clear that the character in the advertising campaign doesn't care about her husband. In the advertisement, he sounds like a fool, a jerk who accepts this bonding pattern, in which money is the strong link to maintaining a relationship. The subliminal idea is that the partner accepts a relationship along the lines of "*fool me, I like it*". Men often tend to choose women for their bodies and their beauty. The reverse is also true, but with subtle differences. Many women look for a handsome, fit man who appears to have money and power. Intelligence, affection, partnership and culture may not be relevant.

If a couple's relationship is based on their sex life, danger is looming! The risk of the relationship collapsing is high, as someone else will soon appear around the couple with more sexual attraction. One factor that makes a relationship consistent is the ability of the partners to be intimate, complicit and truthful about what they feel and think.

Another problem. What will be in the minds of children and young people watching this kind of commercial? They might think things like: "Will I be able to get results when I grow up if I offer my body during difficult times in my married life? Can my body be an instrument of power over men? Do I have to be a beautiful, attractive woman to feel valued?"

It is well known that sexual, physical and moral abuse are factors that lead to mental illness. But verbal abuse and abuse transmitted through images are also harmful.

Faced with the female "outcry", the agency that created the advertisement issued this press release: "*It is obvious that this is a joke and in no way a disparagement of the female figure. The aim is to show that the sensuality of Brazilian women can be an effective weapon when it comes to breaking bad news.*"

Nothing is obvious in life. Jokes also cause great suffering and damage to people's lives. Yes, the commercial suggests the depreciation of women and men. What's worse: the agency says that sensuality can be an effective weapon for bad news. Hello, girls! Give up your studies and sacrifices to become someone else; take a course in how to use sensuality to get ahead in life!

In fact, it's clear that there's only one way to report the news - good or bad - and that's to be truthful, respectful, clear and direct. The rest is a lot of make-believe.

I'm not trying to condemn the advertising agencies. I understand that the creators of the commercial wanted to sell their product, and they tried to do so in a way that would impact the consumer. However, we have to bear in mind that those who are exposed to what comes out of the television often don't have the tools to look more closely at what advertising offers. We live in the age of consumption, and it seems that anything can be done to sell a product. It's not like that. Let's be vigilant!

Interestingly, the men didn't complain about the subliminal content of this advertisement! Perhaps a large part of the male universe looks down on women?

Since it's up to advertising agencies to publicize their work, with a view to the population's consumption, it's up to me, as a psychotherapist, to offer the public what's hidden behind some of these actions. In this way, people will be able to develop the critical capacity not to buy catnip!

DRINKING CAN BECOME A DISEASE - ALCOHOLISM

We psychiatrists have a lot of trouble helping people who use alcohol excessively and end up falling ill as a result. The problem lies in the fact that there are no tests to indicate that the person has become dependent on alcohol - in other words, an alcoholic. There is simply no way of proving to the patient that they already have signs of addiction. There are no blood tests, imaging tests, liver tests or any other method to indicate the disorder.

Another factor that makes it difficult to treat an alcoholic is the fact that they don't feel sick or dependent. You can see how difficult it is to treat someone who doesn't feel ill. Doctors don't have any concrete evidence to show the presence of the disease.

In psychiatry, we don't use the term alchoholic, because this word refers to someone who idolizes alcohol, which is not true in the life of an addict.

If there's a standard behavior among addicts - no matter what they're addicted to - it's the understanding that they can quit at any time. The idea that one is in control (which takes so long to crumble in the addicted mind) is especially strong among alcohol addicts. They believe they are doing nothing wrong when they drink; they believe they are socializing - after all, they drink "socially".

The subterfuges are many and varied. For example: an alcoholic who is given to beer thinks that he is not a problem because he doesn't drink stronger drinks, such as spirits (cachaça, whisky and vodka). In fact, these drinks have a higher alcohol content, but beer does alter the state of consciousness and becomes an addiction in the lives of certain people. On the other hand, those who drink too much wine think they are different from other drinkers, because they are drinking a more sophisticated and expensive beverage.

These are some of the reasons why it is so difficult for professionals, family and friends to show an alcoholic or alcoholic that they have a serious health problem. The person refuses to see what everyone else sees, but there are no precise diagnoses - so medical opinions are subjective and look like mere opinions to the patient.

Those who first notice the problem are also the ones who suffer its consequences most intensely: the addict's family. Fortunately, most people who drink alcohol do not become dependent.

Alcoholism is statistically the most common chemical dependency in the population. In numerical terms, the harmful consequences of alcohol abuse are insurmountable in terms of addiction, violence and direct and indirect deaths, such as in traffic accidents, for example. Damage to social and professional dynamics and turbulence in marital and family relationships are also recurrent. From the point of view of government spending, it beats all other addictions combined.

Why is the use of alcohol so pleasurable? I confess that the first time I had a draft beer, and later a whisky, I found the taste very unpleasant. It's not because it's something delicious, pleasant to the taste buds, that we start drinking it. What alcohol does, in the first place, is alter the state of consciousness in an apparently beneficial way: depending on the user's predisposition, it can make them more sociable, more uninhibited, more shameless, less depressed, less distressed, more relaxed. It makes it easier for insecure people to approach people they are interested in. In short, alcohol helps us to fool ourselves, to deceive ourselves. Over time, some people will only be able to interact socially after drinking.

A clear sign of alcohol dependence is the loss of ability to control the amount you drink after you start drinking. What is this? These are addicts who can go as long as they like without drinking, but who, once they start, don't know how to drink very little. They intend to drink one, two or three cans of beer, but they drink a lot. This is evidence that their relationship with alcohol has become unhealthy.

In these people who lose control, there is an important phenomenon: whenever they try to drink a little, they don't succeed. We have no idea why this happens; even if they don't drink for months, when they come back, they end up drinking a lot. It seems that the continued use of large quantities of alcohol creates a transformation in the brain, leading to a loss of control over how much you drink. Imagine if our body lost control of our thirst and we drank water until we had heart failure?

There are various problems caused by alcohol use, in addition to the dependence described above. There are people who drink very little and then react disproportionately to the amount drunk, becoming aggressive. We call this "pathological intoxication". There are the "heavy" drinkers, those who drink almost daily but who haven't yet lost control of the amount they drink, even though they cause all kinds of havoc in their surroundings.

In fact, alcohol is used by many people as if it were a medicine, as if it were relieving anxiety or nervousness and improving the mood of the most downcast and depressed. Some start drinking because they realize that alcohol helps fight insomnia. Over time, the use of alcohol worsens the quality of sleep, making insomnia worse. These would be the major benefits sought by most heavy drinkers.

Benefits? Actually, harm...

* * *

Let's talk about teenagers' relationship with alcohol. The other day, I saw thousands of teenagers arriving at a big music event on the north coast of Rio Grande do Sul. Perhaps 90% of them were already drunk, carrying spirits before entering the venue. I thought: "Something doesn't add up in my observation. Either the event is of poor quality, or these young people don't feel prepared for these parties." I was left with the second hypothesis.

Do you have to drink a lot to enjoy a party? Of course not. Let's not forget that the parents of these young people are complicit in alcohol abuse. There is always the use of alcohol in some teenager's home before they go out to parties, in the so-called "warm-up".

* * *

There are a few maxims said by alcoholics: "I've never drunk to the point of falling over"; "I don't drink spirits"; "I drink when I want and stop when I want"; "I've never stopped working because of alcohol"; "I drink socially"; "I drink and pay my bills"; "I don't drink in bars". Of course, these are loose phrases that don't detract from these people's dependence on alcohol.

We need to talk about the partners of alcoholics. They often complain a lot about their partners' reactions when they drink, but it's very common for them to drink together. They are therefore complicit and endorse the use of alcohol. I mentioned partners because men still drink more than women. Of course, women are drinking more and more. Perhaps they are trying to feel equal to men, but they are equal to the worst that can exist in some men. This is not female independence, but imprisonment, because they will become weaker and sicker.

* * *

Although the appearance of alcohol consumption - wrapped up in social, pleasant, happy contexts - doesn't recommend any greater caution, it is necessary to pay special attention to alcohol abuse habits. Diagnosis is hazy, treatment is difficult and the course of the disease and its consequences are often tragic.

This is the worst public problem in the area of mental health. It causes incalculable damage to the public purse - worse than that caused by the use of marijuana or even cocaine, because alcohol is socially accepted. You can drink it anywhere. Those who use cocaine are fewer in number than those who use alcohol. Alcoholism also has a genetic basis, i.e. the risk of offspring becoming alcoholics increases if there is a disease in the ancestors.

Dependence on alcohol takes years, while dependence on cocaine and *crack* cocaine is very fast. I say this to show that alcoholics have a longer time to build up some assets, get married and have children. However, with the presence of the disease, everything begins to collapse: professional career, family, assets, mental health and family harmony. Cocaine addicts are younger people who, due to the presence of the disease, are unable to build anything in their lives and generally depend on their parents to get by.

There are no medications that take away the urge to drink. We have medicines that cause unpleasant effects for the patient if they are taken with drink. They can make you feel nauseous, give you a headache, redden your face and make your heart race. We call them "aversive" to alcohol. They should not be given secretly, without the patient's knowledge.

Treatment aims to show the patient how much their life has been compromised by alcohol use. Of course, the family's role in treatment is fundamental, as the disease affects everyone. Even if the alcoholic doesn't want to seek help, it's recommended that the family go and tell them that they will continue, even if they don't join the treatment. In cases where the patient's life is seriously compromised, hospitalization may be the only way forward, even if the patient doesn't want it.

Alcohol use can cause psychotic symptoms, such as exaggerated suspicions, unhealthy jealousy, physical aggression and hallucinations (hearing voices or seeing things that aren't there). The risk of suicide is higher among alcoholics, as alcohol use increases depression.

There is a common situation that arises from excessive alcohol use: the so-called memory *blackout*. The person doesn't remember what they did when they were drunk. Sometimes they lose things, attack people, spend too much... I've seen a guy in a mental institution who killed a friend while drunk and couldn't remember that it had happened. How many of you have had your memory erased by alcohol?

* * *

Finally: imagine someone having a heart attack and not feeling any symptoms. They'd die, right? That's the problem with our alcoholics. They don't feel sick. How do you treat someone who doesn't feel sick? Difficult, but knowing more about this disease and having the family involved can make a difference.

The treatments that give the best results are not those carried out solely in the offices of psychiatrists and psychologists, but those carried out in conjunction with Alcoholics Anonymous (AA) and its family groups (Al Anon).

HOW TO RETAIN TALENTED PROFESSIONALS

We now realize that professionals no longer dream only of a career in one company, as was the case a few years ago. The most talented, due to their high qualifications, tend not to stay in the same job for long. Is this new model of employment only related to the salary received? No. The security of those who have the best training makes them want to seek out new opportunities in order to acquire more and more knowledge.

Is there any way to keep professionals in institutions for longer?

Yes, there are other ways. Well, I'll start by saying that there are other procedures that should be part of the company's human resources policy, which give priority to the professional's training and experience, providing opportunities for advancement within the company.

I was asked this question in one of the lectures I gave at TECNOPUC (Technology Center of the Pontifical Catholic University of Rio Grande do Sul). I surprise businesspeople with the points I make about the emotional problems that interfere with careers and that are little appreciated and known in companies.

First comes transparency. You have to be truthful, clear and not mince your words when communicating with your employees. And this must be a two-way street. It is essential that the manager, the leader, in short, makes it very clear to their team everything that concerns work, how to deal with routine business situations and the possibilities and expectations that each person can nurture within the company. Likewise, employees must be encouraged to feel at ease, to the point where they can communicate clearly, objectively, truthfully and openly, without risk of reprisals, even if they communicate in a politically incorrect way.

This is better for the health of the environment, those involved and, ultimately, the company's finances. This way, employees get involved in a real project, in something that makes sense to everyone and is worth leaving home to work for.

I would also highlight involvement. Look around you, in your work environment. Do you really know the people you work with? If you think about it, you'll know that the answer is "no". If you're an employee in an organization, think about it and try to take an interest in your colleagues. With greater complicity and affinity, this will do them good, but also you and the environment as a whole. Now, if you're a manager, you should seek an attitude of interest and involvement. Of course, I'm not suggesting that the company should become a psychologist's office. However, that model of cold, serial production will not bring good results. People seek fulfillment and well-being and they will only find them in places where they feel really important, where they are truly involved by their leaders.

We often ask people: "How are you?". We expect them to answer: "Fine", in protocol. However, if you look closely at the other person, you can see in their facial expressions some indication of their real mood. If you notice something, you can say: "Wow, you look good! That's good!"; or: "Listen, I can see that you're distressed, distant, with a look of suffering and worry. Has something happened? Do you want to talk?". There is truth in this and closer bonds will emerge. The other person feels important.

Would you, as a manager, tell your employees that you are willing and able to listen to them, even if they disagree with your attitude? Would you open up your schedule to any employee, without the risk of punishing them if you didn't like what you heard? I don't think many would fit that profile. There are always obstacles between those who manage and those they manage.

Respect is also non-negotiable. It's common for people to use their superior hierarchical position to express their views on things without worrying about how they express their opinions, which can lead to hurt feelings and discontent. If a manager is rude, angry or threatening to his subordinate, even if something inappropriate has been generated by the employee, this attitude will lead to resentment and distance. The attitude and response of the person who has been insulted can be unpredictable. The best way to express our discomfort and displeasure is through words. However, few people have the ability to talk to others. The vast majority react with irritation, aggression, or remain silent - but they will make sure they get their comeuppance.

If you, the manager, have a more forceful complaint for an employee, talk to him or her in private. It's not healthy to reprimand in public. Also be careful not to be the manager who sends messages via third parties, or you won't be respected in the institution.

Now think with me. Let's talk about **recognition**. How many times have you complained about someone in the last few days? Probably several. And how many times recently have you praised someone and offered recognition for their achievements? I'll bet few times, or none at all. That's the pattern. We complain a lot and recognize little. It's part of a competitive and productive life, in which we all have many interests and little time to talk. But we need to stop, look around and know how to praise. There's no need to lie, force or invent.

As we are hired to get things right, to fulfill our obligations, our successes are often not appreciated. And it's the mistakes that get the attention. However, the good manager or productive and engaging leader, from whom the employee will not want to part, knows how to offer merit and support at all times, both in success and in misfortune.

Would you, CEO, director, go to the hospital to visit a subordinate as a token of your care and attention? Or would you go to the funeral of the father or mother of an employee who wasn't in the top echelon?

The use of truth is fundamental to establishing and developing mature, responsible and committed relationships in any type of interpersonal relationship. We find it very difficult to be truthful with people, because we come up against fantasies and fears that others might be offended by the truth. I have no doubt that managers who are truthful will be more remembered and admired by their employees. This is also a way of retaining talent.

Note that I haven't mentioned money so far. The financial incentive is the most automatic and simple answer to the question posed at the beginning of this reflection. Of course it's important, it counts. However, as expensive as it may be, money is something that all companies have to offer. If the competition for a professional is limited to money, then the best-capitalized will win. But it is possible to balance the situation with other incentives, with less obvious but more solid rewards.

We all want higher salaries and better financial conditions, but feeling recognized, welcomed and with prospects for personal and professional growth are advantages that no amount of money can buy. On the other hand, an employee who works only for the money will be a dissatisfied person who is unlikely to commit to their work environment. This concept applies to any activity in life. Anything done solely for financial gain runs the risk of never leading anywhere.

Perhaps it would be worthwhile, in a company with many employees, for leaders to invite employees from all levels to a private conversation, or even in small groups. On this occasion, they should be asked to talk about the company, what they think of their work, if they have any suggestions to offer, if they are satisfied. If this strategy is difficult to implement, another way of listening to them would be through anonymous forms, in which they could talk about the company.

The best way to keep good professionals is to really care about people and genuinely get close to them. It's very seductive to offer extra perks and benefits to your employees - something that's out of the ordinary and that the company can offer at a time when it's making more money.

There is an understanding that the good employee is not doing anything that is not their duty, so they don't deserve praise. That's not right. It's like a strict parent telling their child that getting a ten at school isn't something to be praised for, because it's their duty. Discouraging, right?

Yes, everything that is done with care, attention, dedication and that brings benefits deserves praise. Even an occasional bad result may not be cause for criticism. It's important to realize and record that the person did their best, regardless of the return achieved.

WHIP THERAPY

Don't be alarmed by the title of this article, as it is somewhat caricatured. I'm relating an instrument used by the gauchos of the pampas to a psychotherapeutic approach. The clapper, lash or whip is used to beat the horse when it doesn't follow the instructions of its tamer.

Human beings have a strong tendency to mistreat themselves and put themselves down. We turn everyday events and disagreements into guilt and resentment, when we don't develop miraculous remorse. As much as it hurts to hear criticism from others, we don't spare ourselves from voracious and merciless self-criticism. We live in a battle against this spirit of self-flagellation, always reaffirming in the mirror that we are not capable, that we are not good enough for this or that. We constantly believe that others see us in the same diminished way, that our parents don't pay attention to us, that our spouse doesn't value us, that our boss doesn't give us any prestige. We find it very difficult to absorb flattering words. It's very easy to objectify ourselves.

It's clear that this behavior, so common in our species, is a major obstacle. One of the great specialties of our **art of being unhappy**.

I'm taking the liberty of describing a story I witnessed in my office, with my patient's agreement. Of course, I'm distorting the story and not revealing any information that could identify the person.

He specialized in boycotting, putting himself down and disqualifying himself. He was a PhD in these subjects. We'd start talking and he'd start talking badly about himself, belittling himself and thinking he was the sole reason for all his problems. According to his own concept, he was no good at anything. His way of being showed his sadness, dejection and lack of spirit. His air was heavy. He considered himself a *bag without* a *handle*. It couldn't be any other way.

He was in a very desperate situation. He had always used various medications, but without satisfactory results. In fact, in situations like this, medication helps little or nothing, because the suffering is more existential than biochemical. There were times when I felt powerless to help this patient. Our meetings resembled a struggle, in which I pointed out alternatives to his difficulties, but he dismissed them, as if nothing made sense in my interventions. I could see that he was unconsciously trying to bring himself down, in other words, that I would get tired and abandon him, as if I were powerless to help him. By the way: he had already been to several therapists.

In fact, I felt a certain ambivalence between continuing with him or leaving his life. This kind of stance also meant that he tried to control me; in other words, he tried to take away my strength as his therapist. As he didn't allow my interventions to bear fruit, he ended up disqualifying me, weakening me. Of course, these are unconscious coping mechanisms of this type of person, who doesn't realize what a damaging way to live. Imagine his relationship with his family and other people around him.

One day, faced with his endless complaints, I had a flash of insight outside the academic context of psychoanalytic theories. As this patient constantly abused himself and wouldn't get out of this role, it occurred to me to say to him:

- We're at an impasse: I don't see that I've been able to help you and I'd like to propose another therapeutic approach. To do this, I'd like you to buy a whip or a lash.

He was surprised by my suggestion. He thought I was joking, but I explained the motivation.

"I realize that you have an unhealthy habit of constantly judging yourself, with disqualifying thoughts that haunt you day and night and make you sick. We can change the course of this pathological ritual of yours. You can't escape this self-aggression of your thoughts. Do you agree?"

He replied:

"Yes, I agree."

"Then, whenever you start this aggressive ritual, I'll pretend to take the whip and beat you on the legs. Faced with the discomfort of the abuse, you'll be able to run away from me and, in this way, you won't be molested, flogged. You can't get away from your evil thoughts and self-flagellations, they repeat themselves in your daily life. Maybe that will change."

I ran the risk of losing him if he took offense at my proposal. But he had presence of mind. He bought the whip and gave it to me as a present.

The aim of this **Bagé analyst-style** intervention was to confront him with the obsessive workings of his mind in order to disqualify him and, consequently, make him ill. Whenever he started this litany of mistreating himself, I would point to the lash and he would stop talking. Sometimes he laughed. At that moment, he had an opportunity to look at the way he constructed his thoughts and then try to change them.

* * *

It would be very healthy if we had a friend, family member, spouse, colleague, someone by our side to warn us when we are creating situations that cause us loss and suffering as a result of these emotional conflicts. It wouldn't have to be with a whip, but with words, with some gesture, in short. The fact is that we don't usually notice this way of living, so an outside eye can help. Nobody is born with low self-esteem. This habit of belittling oneself will inevitably lead to depression and paralysis in the face of life.

* * *

I also want to share with you another aspect of this person's psychic functioning: the **feeling of grandeur**. That's right! It may not seem like it, but because of the apparent self-deprecation, this type of sufferer is very grandiose, egocentric and self-centered. After all, they believe that they are the reason for all the problems in their daily lives, as if they were so powerful. They perceive themselves to be so powerful that they blame all of life's difficulties on themselves.

Because it is a megalomaniacal stance, the therapist listens little to their interlocutors. The less experienced therapist runs the risk of not helping, because the feeling of grandiosity prevents the person from listening and absorbing the professional's interventions.

Through examples from everyday life, such as in this article, I want to alert you to how psychologically ill we can become and not have the slightest idea of where it comes from.

CONSIDERATIONS ON THE USE OF LITHIUM

There are many chemical elements in nature. You may remember chemistry lessons, the periodic table. Some elements are abundant, others are rare, many are valuable. And some are widely used. Among them is lithium, which has a variety of applications - from weapons to technological instruments to medicinal products.

In the last century, lithium was even used to find a treatment for tuberculosis. It didn't bring any benefits in terms of curing the disease. However, researchers noticed that patients with advanced tuberculosis and no chance of survival improved their mood with the use of lithium. As a result of this chance discovery, the element began to be used in psychiatry to treat mood disorders.

Lithium is not addictive. It can be used for years without risk of addiction. It doesn't make you dopey or prevent you from doing your day-to-day activities, such as driving a car or even flying an airplane. The main precautions for those who use it should be in relation to the kidneys and thyroid. Laboratory tests are recommended to assess these two organs. Frequent complaints from those who use this medication are hand tremors, increased appetite and diarrhea.

Among the many questions I receive from patients, one in particular catches my attention. People often come to me saying that, after taking a blood test, their doctor has told them that their lithium level is low, which is why they suffer from depression, are moody and sad and therefore need to replenish this element.

In fact, science reveals that lithium levels are extremely low in all human beings. It doesn't matter how much lithium we have in our blood. The laboratory indication of the level of lithium in the blood is of absolutely no use when it comes to psychiatric illnesses. Psychiatrists are only interested in blood lithium levels when they use lithium-based drugs to treat mood disorders.

These disorders include depression and bipolar disorder. Statistics show that the number of patients with depression alone is higher than those with bipolar disorder.

When a person is euphoric, excited, explosive and irritable, causing agitation and excessive activity, talking too much, spending too much and having too much energy, we call it mania. When the individual is apathetic, sad, discouraged, tearful and lacks energy, we call it **depression**.

Taking lithium is not an indication that a person has a bad head or is crazy, as some people claim. Lithium is a mood moderator and is the gold standard medication for treating mood disorders worldwide. Its best effect is in patients with euphoria and agitation, but it is also indicated for those who only have depression. In the latter case, it should be combined with antidepressants. Lithium also reduces the risk of suicide in depressed patients.

Returning to the question of lithium in the blood, it must be clear that no one is depressed because of a lack of this element in their bloodstream. Otherwise, you'd just have to replace the lithium and that would be that. Such a conclusion, encouraged by some ill-informed professionals, will lead to confusion and misdirection of this possible psychiatric disorder. It only makes sense to know the level of lithium in the blood after the patient has taken the lithium-based medication. Doctors assess whether the dosage in the blood is therapeutic or whether it may be higher than desired and could intoxicate the patient.

Homeopathic medicines usually have very low dosages of lithium, so they don't help in the treatment of psychiatric illnesses.

EMOTIONAL SUFFERING AS PROTECTION

Here I present an interesting and worrying aspect of the workings of our unconscious or emotional system. When patients suffer from depressive or anxious symptoms, we psychiatrists need to investigate the origins of the problem. This investigation is indispensable because it will help us make a decision - whether to medicate the patient or suggest psychotherapy or, even better, whether both therapeutic approaches are appropriate at the same time.

It's interesting to see how people deal with the demands of everyday life. I'm talking about things like the need to perform, support oneself, work, study, date, marry, have children, separate, etc. Faced with these demands and the difficulties that life imposes, some people may experience a certain type of suffering or psychiatric symptom. These symptoms include depression, lack of energy, apathy, discouragement, sadness, loss of interest, insomnia, nervousness, irritability, lack or excess of appetite, anxiety... I'm talking here about people who had no history of psychiatric illness, who had been going about their lives normally, but who, faced with some major obstacle, ended up falling ill.

These symptoms usually appear in a sneaky way, apparently taking the person by surprise. Once present, they solidify to the point where they bring limitations and suffering into the patient's life. These depressive or anxious symptoms, built up unconsciously by the mind, can serve as a shield, an alibi to keep us away from the commitments, challenges and obligations that life presents us with. It's not something designed or planned by the individual's head, but they are traps and pitfalls created by the individual themselves - and which will inevitably make them develop in the art of being unhappy.

The impression is that feeling bad gives the subject a certain protection. But this is only an apparent shelter, a refuge. The fact is that this shield of suffering deprives us of confrontations and the simplest possible achievements

- and even the most laborious and exhausting feats. Imagine a bulletproof vest that, when analyzed, turns out to be an ordinary vest with Styrofoam protection. This is what this neurotic pseudo-shield created by these people is like: although it gives a feeling of security, deep down it only exposes and weakens the person. It's a shield that appears to protect us, but deprives us of everything. It's a trapdoor that's always in our way, set up by ourselves.

In this context, the patient feels depressed and seeks medical help. The psychiatrist is expected to prescribe antidepressants. What is often observed is that there is no improvement with the drugs taken. Of course, the problem is not the quality or efficiency of the antidepressants. The problem is that it's a suffering of the mind, of the soul - and the medicine doesn't touch it. We are dealing with a pilgrim patient, who goes from office to office, looking for more medication for his problems.

This patient imagines that he has no cure. They see their situation as irrevocable, literally irremediable, because they believe they have already done everything, tried every possible form of treatment. They feel and look as if they are truly condemned, in a chronic state. As a result, he becomes more and more depressed and distressed. It is, in fact, a vicious circle. Your life comes to a standstill, it becomes unfeasible - and this in all its various spheres: love, family, social, professional and sporting.

If anxiety-related symptoms predominate, the course of the illness can lead to fears and phobias about even the simplest activities - going to certain places, traveling, leaving the house, etc. There are even cases of panic disorder. We are subjected to this in various ways, with very different intensities and consequences. But the bottom line is one and the same: unidentified and, consequently, unresolved emotional conflicts.

Treatments are laborious and difficult, because it's not easy to get rid of these symptoms. At the same time as they make you suffer, they also protect you.

* * *

A lady felt depressed and used various psychiatric drugs, but she didn't get any better. Her family wanted a second opinion, so they came to me. When I spoke to her, I couldn't see any neurochemical context to explain her depression. What's more, she had been taking a series of drugs without any therapeutic success. After a while, I realized that her husband was demanding that she go to work, which she didn't want to do.

In short, her depression served as a shield so that her husband would stop demanding work from her. As her husband was accompanying her, I asked permission to call him to her appointment. She asked me not to tell him about the idea of depression as a "shield". I felt that my perception made sense.

* * *

I remember a young man whose parents wanted him to study abroad, following the path of his two older brothers. The younger one was very attached to his mother and always feared a separation, which would happen if he left the country. The young man then began to develop fears of leaving home, had symptoms of gastritis and a lack of appetite, losing weight, leading him to undergo various tests, all of which were normal.

I could clearly see that the young man had practically developed the symptoms to protect himself from the challenges he would have to face. He didn't reveal that he wasn't going to travel, but his mind was signaling that he was ill and wouldn't be able to carry out the task his parents wanted him to do. The possibility of getting better, of getting well, would throw him into something he didn't want to do.

Realize that there is no medication that can cure this illness. Psychotherapy would be the only way to clarify the reasons for their illness. Of course, the healthiest thing would be to be able to verbalize, to consciously and objectively oppose your parents' plan. Even if the plan to spend some time away wasn't a bad one, it would be a case of choice. Being honest with yourself and your parents was fundamental.

* * *

Realize that removing the symptom, improving the person, is no easy task. If we could magically solve these patients' symptoms, there would certainly be other suffering. Psychotherapists who don't have this clear perception won't help their patients. The figure of the shield, created by the mind, serves to protect the person from something that causes them discomfort. It is still a form of "power", in the sense that the patient imposes their will, even in this disguised way.

Realize how easily we lose ourselves in the art of being unhappy.

HOW TO HELP CHILDREN PROTECT THEMSELVES FROM PEDOPHILES

You'll notice from the title that this article isn't about us protecting children, but helping them to defend themselves and avoid pedophilia. Of course, we must always protect children from threats to their physical and mental health. However, my idea here is to offer tools so that children themselves are not taken by surprise when faced with a brutal act that is completely unknown to their imagination.

Pedophilia. This is a very delicate subject. It is defined as sexual attraction to children and pubescents who have not yet developed secondary sexual characteristics, such as pubic hair, breasts, etc. We don't even like to contemplate the issue because we don't understand the horror of this practice, and also because we don't want to think of the children in our relationships as victims of it. However, this is a real problem that must be faced. More than that: we need to understand the habits and methods of pedophiles, so that we can guide children not to fall for their tricks.

There are many awareness campaigns, government actions, victim support associations, in short, various institutions committed to combating pedophilia and dealing with its consequences. It is an action that emerges from the sick unconscious of an adult. There is not the slightest possibility of our imagination understanding, justifying and accepting this conduct. It's easier to assimilate murder than child abuse. That's why I ask:

Can you talk about pedophilia and try to help the child?

We need to be direct, guiding prevention and strategies to try to avoid this violence. Yes, we must deal with the victims, but we must urgently act preventively so that fewer children become victims of pedophilia. And this can be done through simple, clear and honest communication between parents and children. From an early age, as soon as children consciously understand what they are being told, we should explain that there is a possibility that older people (teenagers, adults and the elderly) will want to get too close, with more or less subtle touching and abuse.

Of course, there is no best age to start talking about the subject. However, children between the ages of three and four are usually able to understand what we're talking about. In other words, warnings against pedophilia should start very early and stop very late, only when the young person has enough discernment to act and react on their own.

Why do parents find it difficult to broach this subject with their children? Perhaps out of embarrassment, or because they don't value the issue enough, or because they confuse these teachings with things related to sex, as if they were going to arouse children's early interest in the subject. I think adults have a lot of taboos about sexual life, so they can't see the simplicity in talking to children.

There can be more silence on the subject when people are very religious. They tend to associate sex with sin, which leads to more resistance on the subject of pedophilia. I've noticed that adults deny the possibility of it happening in their family, so they dismiss the possibility of raising the subject. Others think it's better not to raise the subject, as it could stimulate the child's curiosity about sex. This is how they reason: "What is not seen is not remembered..."

I repeat: conversations with children must be clear, simple, truthful and direct. A good strategy is to always ask the child how their day was when they get home from their activities. If they enjoyed it, if they had a fight with someone, if someone mistreated them, if something happened, if something made them sad. This simple daily exercise can leave the door open for children to talk.

Here are some suggestions for advice to give to children:

"Don't let anyone touch your body."

"Don't let anyone take your clothes off."

"Don't let anyone touch your sexual organs."

"Don't stand near an adult who takes their clothes off."

"Don't obey if someone tells you to touch your body."

"In all these cases, if it happens, if someone tries something, refuse, get away. If you have to, shout, run."

"If something like that happens, go home and talk to your mother or father."

If we don't talk to the children beforehand, they will be very frightened by an act committed by a pedophile. And they will tend not to tell us for two reasons. Firstly, because of a threat from the pedophile himself. This is because aggressors always play on the child's fear. Little ones believe it when someone says: "If you tell anyone what I did to you, I'll kill you", "If you tell anyone, I'll kill your mother". As they are threatened, they imagine that they have done something very wrong and that if they tell their parents, they will be punished in some way.

Overcome the embarrassment and talk openly with your children, because there's no point in pretending the problem doesn't exist. And this care must be unceasing, because we are surrounded by potential pedophiles, since we never know who they really are. In other words, the habit of pedophilia is one of the most hidden. The pedophile is concealed, disguised, so it is very difficult to predict his attack, because you don't know where it will come from. Therefore, you have to be constantly careful. Generally, the aggressor is someone very close to the child, a relative, friend or neighbor. So it's someone the family trusts.

It's worth remembering that children touching each other's bodies is not considered pedophilia, but rather a way of discovering each other and realizing their anatomical similarities and differences. We shouldn't look at these games as something reprehensible or sick. Remember that children touch each other, but without the evil of adult thought and gaze.

In order to encourage verbal interaction, parents need to encourage children when they want to talk about anything in the house. We see many parents disqualifying their children's speech, which prevents them from telling what is happening or what they think.

So it makes all the difference for children to know that they can always tell their parents everything. Children who have listened to their parents' recommendations not to let anyone touch their bodies will be free to tell them if anything happens. However, some parents may react inappropriately, sometimes even blaming the child for the violence they have been subjected to. They may insinuate that their child supposedly gave them the slip, facilitating or even provoking the aggressor. Sometimes they criticize the type of clothes the girl was wearing, as if this justified the pedophile's actions.

* * *

What can society and the judiciary do to try to change the behavior of pedophiles? On the part of the authorities, what is on offer is the imprisonment of the pedophile, which obviously won't bring about any change in his perverse thinking and impulses. It doesn't help to just lock them up, because no prisoner stays in Brazilian jails for long. He'll soon get out and be terminated.

However, the only solution that actually brings results is **chemical** castration. The person is injected with a medication that inhibits the production of testosterone, leading to a loss of sexual desire. As well as solving the cases of active pedophiles, this procedure would also be educational, as it would serve as an inhibiting example for potential pedophiles.* Of course, this procedure would have to be monitored by the judiciary.

Psychotherapy is not required by pedophiles. The big problem we face is that pedophiles don't perceive themselves to be ill or distressed by their behavior. Psychiatry has no clear explanation, from a psychological point of view, for the perverse behavior of these people.

---

* Editor's note: Bill number 5398/2013 (authored by Jair Bolsonaro, a federal deputy from Rio de Janeiro) is currently being processed in the National Congress, which, according to the text, "Increases the penalty for the crimes of rape and rape of a vulnerable person, requires that those convicted of these crimes complete voluntary chemical treatment to inhibit sexual desire as a requirement for obtaining conditional release and regime progression" (emphasis added).

In my experience as a psychotherapist, I can't remember any pedophiles who came to me because they were guilty as a result of their sexual impulses. I only came to them when they were involved in legal proceedings. In those cases, the interest was in getting out of jail, not in treating the perversion. Look how complicated it is to deal with these sick people. I'm not calling them criminals, although their conduct is criminal.

THE IMPORTANCE OF TRUTH IN RELATIONSHIPS

Life is one big make-believe. A theater.

Look. Notice how difficult it is to hear and speak the strict truth of things. Think about your relationships and you'll remember how we are constantly giving and receiving excuses, justifications, ponderations and even untruths. At various levels of verisimilitude, we are proficient at modulating the discourse, moving more or less away from the truth of what is being said.

It goes for everything.

When we're late: "Look, the traffic was heavy", "I had an unexpected setback...". Not that these justifications can't be true from time to time, but in general, traffic, setbacks and other factors are at most mitigating elements for our disorganization, unwillingness to be at a place at the agreed time or even just disregard for others. Why not just tell the truth? "Look, I'm sorry, I got caught up in my appointments and I ended up missing the time"; "I left late and I was late"; "I forgot my appointment. I'm sorry...".

Or, when we want to disagree with someone about something, we often resort to unnecessary mitigating factors: "With all due respect... Look... I ask you to understand me and I apologize for anything, but I have to say that you may be mistaken..." Well, that's a lot of turns, a lot of reticence. We introduce and apologize more beforehand than we say. This takes the focus away from the problem we want to address and weakens our argument in the eyes of the interlocutor. Why not simply and politely address the problem directly? "Look, I think you're not handling this situation well and you could improve on this and that. I'm also going to re-evaluate my participation. What do you think?"

It doesn't mean that we have to be rude and that we don't need to care about how we communicate. That would be excess, the opposite of those flourishes and fears that take us away from the truth and the solution to issues. After all, rather than proving that we're on the right track and that the other person is wrong, we should want resolutions, definitions and well-being. There's also no point in being right but in disharmony or discomfort. So let's take the middle path, with sufficient care, with kindness - but without running away from the point of the conversation.

Prudence is necessary. And this should not be confused with cowardice, which is an extrapolation of prudence. Cowardice, fear and trepidation make us lie or evade the core of the issue at hand. We invent excuses and justifications to mitigate situations. In general (I would say almost all the time), we don't speak the truth, we aren't clear, because we fear the other person's response to our statement. As we build up our thoughts about what to say and how to say it to our interlocutor, we can get in the way and stall as we worry about their response. This is the great trap that can mute or distort a thought or a sentence.

However, we can't be reckless either - which is the other extrapolation of prudence. This other exaggeration, this other extreme, is a lack of awareness about what and how things should be said. This recklessness leads us to what I call **sincericide**.

Let's look at all this in the professional environment.

Your boss asks you what you think of an idea he had, of a project he presented to you and your colleagues. You didn't like it for various reasons. What do you say? Even if they're absolutely disgusted and annoyed, it's normal for people to say something like: "That sounds like a good idea. It'll work!" We've seen it at work. And it always sounds false, it's always fake, forced and even embarrassing for others, because only a very talented actor would be able to contradict themselves without letting it show. But we could also hear: "Look, that's a terrible idea! There's no way I'm going to do that. It won't work at all!"

With the first form, the cowardly and lying form, we reveal falsehood and lose the respect of our boss and colleagues. The second way, the reckless and sincere way, reveals inflexibility, selfishness and a lack of practical sense.

Much better for everyone would be to stick to the truth in content, but with politeness, clarity and care in form. Something like this: "Well, I understand your good intentions, but I think there are problems here and there. If we do *this instead*, perhaps the result will be better. What do you think?" This is how we show interest, respect and honesty.

* * *

Another everyday sincericide is to meet a friend you haven't seen for years and say: "How you've aged"; or: "How fat you are!"

* * *

Recently, a patient asked me at the end of a consultation: "Do you want me to pay you?" I looked at him, thought and then fell silent. After a few seconds - which for him must have been an eternity - he came back to me: "Doctor, you haven't answered me." As I have an agreement with all my patients about how we pay for my services, I didn't see the need to reply and preferred to let him realize what he was doing. I just said, "You don't seem to want to pay me today!" To which he said: "Yes, you're right. The thing is, I don't have any money on me and I forgot my checkbook at home. Can I pay you next week?" Of course he could. I showed him the risk of not being clear, objective and not telling the truth.

* * *

It's very common for patients to be repeatedly late for their appointments and to apologize. I often ask them why they are formally apologizing. They reply that it's out of consideration for me, politeness, etc. Well, they're not on time because they've paid more attention to something else that's taken up their time. So I show them that they don't need to apologize, because it was a choice they made and it resulted in them being late with me. Of course, I don't feel diminished by this; however, I would prefer it if they didn't say anything at all, instead of making some excuse.

* * *

I once told one of those patients with lame excuses that I'd rather he told me he'd met a friend on the way and would rather have coffee with him than come to the appointment. That would be fine with me, because he had taken an action that suited him at the time. Of course, in the next session, I would explore this change of route further...

* * *

I remember something else. An acquaintance waved to me from across the street and made a point of crossing. I stopped and he crossed the street. When he got close, he tapped me on the shoulder and said: "I think you're in a hurry. Go on..." I realized he must be in a hurry and replied: "I'm not in a hurry, I stopped to talk to you. I think you're in a hurry." I thought that perhaps he didn't want to talk to me. It did me good to offer him my perception of what was going on.

* * *

It's not uncommon for young children to overhear their parents arguing in an exaggerated, high-pitched manner and then ask the following question: "Are you fighting?". What do they usually hear in response? "No, we were just talking about something unimportant." But it would be better to say: "Yes, we're discussing some problems. I'm sorry we were shouting, but don't be alarmed, we won't be shouting any more in the next discussion. We'll talk in a way that won't scare you."

* * *

It's good to stress that we can also offer the truth about attitudes, ideas and feelings that we like about the other person. We can say that we like what someone has done, how they put themselves forward, that they are important in our lives, that it's good to share experiences and time, that they are intelligent, etc.

I think that what makes it difficult for people to offer what they really feel and think to their interlocutors is the fear of the other person's reaction, of the response. When we give our opinion or ask questions, it's essential that we keep the following assumption in mind: we have no idea what the other person's reaction will be, so we have to know that this is how relationships work. Be true to your perceptions and try to offer them with respect, affection and attention. Whenever we keep our words and feelings under wraps, we end up paying for it. Anxiety, irritation and stress can occur in the face of experiences that have not been well elaborated.

But no sincericide either! You'll appreciate yourself more if you can offer the truth. Of course, your truth, your feelings. It's not a question of right or wrong, but of giving the other person what you're feeling and perceiving. Of course, in many situations, silence is the best delivery. Life doesn't have to be a big theater.

THE MANY MASKS OF DEPRESSION

The World Health Organization estimates that by the year 2025 depression will be the second most common disease in the world, second only to cardiovascular disease.

People find it difficult to realize that they may be depressed. In our culture, we tend to put everyday factors (real facts of life) behind the signs of depression. On the other hand, even doctors still don't diagnose the illness properly, generally excluding psychiatrists. There is also public prejudice against mental illness. This means that patients don't think about depression, because psychiatric illnesses are seen as something for weak and incompetent people. As if it were a "freshness", something for the idle.

Depression is one of the mood disorders. They used to be called affective disorders. Imagine our mood fluctuating. When it moves downwards, it would be depression; upwards, exaltation, euphoria, accelerated thinking and agitation. When the mood swings both ways, we call it bipolar disorder. In the majority of patients with this syndrome, the mood is more downwards, leading to depression rather than bipolar disorder.

The origins of depression can be different. There is depression linked to genetic and family characteristics - in other words, an illness that is passed on to descendants. Of course, there is almost always an external factor that triggers the symptoms. It may not be a very relevant fact in the eyes of others, but for a person with a predisposition, it's enough to make them ill.

Another cause of depression is traumatic experiences: going hungry; witnessing parents fighting and hitting each other in childhood; experiencing the premature death of parents, children or siblings; being sexually abused in childhood; having nowhere to live; not having work or money to support oneself or one's family. It is worth remembering that chronic physical illnesses such as arthritis, hypothyroidism, diabetes, autoimmune diseases and others also lead to depression.

Psychic or emotional conflicts are among the factors that generate depression. They are subjective or unconscious experiences that the person has experienced in a real way or even just in their imagination. I don't want to disqualify the power of these stimuli, even though they may be irrelevant for some people.

It's interesting for a psychotherapist to seek to understand these sources of discouragement, which can prevent a person from getting on with their life. It's this group that I want to explore further. Would it occur to you that some symptoms of psychic origin, such as depression or anxiety, could bring some kind of protection or pseudo-benefit to the depressed patient? You're probably thinking "I'm out of my mind".

There is an understanding in psychiatry that having symptoms of psychic origin can generate some gain for the person. We call this "secondary gain". For example: the person has been taken off work, receiving state welfare benefits because of a health problem; they may be afraid of being discharged and being forced to return to a job they don't like. The unconscious decision to feel bad may help them not to have to go back to work.

Another example. The marriage is going badly. The husband works in another city and when he comes home at the weekend he usually finds his wife depressed, in bed. In her husband's absence, she doesn't show such despondency. In this way, through her symptoms, she puts up a barrier so that she doesn't have to have a sexual relationship.

Another case. A depressed client of mine blamed his condition on his wife's desire to separate. She hadn't left home yet because of his depression. His wife despised him, didn't pay any attention to him and didn't want to have a sex life. Even though he understood the real situation, he wanted me to call his wife and tell her not to leave him, because that would make his depression worse. It sounds hilarious, but it's tragic! I then worked to show him that what he feared - separation - could well be his redemption. Without the source of his sadness, which was his unsuccessful marriage, this man could lead an emotionally healthier life. However, being depressed left him with an apparent power over his wife.

In the three cases reported here, there is one thing in common. It seems that the presence of depression, which in itself equals suffering, also offers a certain protection, an "unconscious alibi" for obtaining a benefit. I hope that anyone depressed reading this article doesn't want to stone me in the public square. I insist with the necessary caveat: this situation is not the result of a conscious plan on the part of the person to take advantage of their condition; rather, it is an unconscious mechanism that occurs outside the patient's will.

In any case, regardless of the causes of depression, the clinical picture requires the same care. But you need to understand where the problem comes from in order to know how to treat it. That's why I emphasize the idea of the **various faces of** depression. These are types that apparently have the same symptoms and result in the same consequences for patients, but the treatments will be very different.

The most obvious distinction between the two is the outcome of antidepressant use. In cases of depression with a biological background, a deficiency of neurotransmitters, due to serious traumas in life or where elements of heredity and chronic physical illnesses are present, treatment with medication brings good results. In the case of depression of an emotional origin, psychotherapy is more effective, as it gives patients the tools to understand their conflicts and change them.

When depression has stronger emotional triggers and we only use antidepressants, without indicating concomitant psychotherapy, we run the risk of not helping the patient, who tends not to get better. The reaction of a clinical doctor, less experienced and unaccustomed to the nuances of psychiatry, in his eagerness to help, is to change medication or try other drugs.

In these cases, the patient may feel that their depression is serious or that there's no cure, since they've taken a lot of medication and haven't improved. Clinicians, cardiologists, neurologists, gynecologists and other colleagues are doctors who prescribe more antidepressants than psychiatrists themselves.

I'm not criticizing this, because I think that many patients won't see a psychiatrist, so it's good that other colleagues can also try to treat them.

A psychiatrist faced with a depressed person is expected to consider prescribing antidepressants. Why is that? Because it will at least serve as a therapeutic test. This is because these medications need to be taken for at least a month to see if they will help. Medical literature shows that patients who take medication and undergo psychotherapy are much more likely to improve.

We need to understand the subtleties of emotions. Without this, we live entangled in the traps we set for ourselves. There are patients who spend their lives changing their medication, trying out new drugs. Perhaps the most appropriate thing would be for them to see a psychotherapist for an assessment and, if necessary, start psychotherapy. It goes without saying that when we suffer from emotional problems, we all hope for a magic remedy that will cure us. Unfortunately, there is no such magic. In order to heal the pains of our soul, it is always essential to be more intimate with our way of being and relating.

It's all very subtle, but that's what a real psychotherapist must be prepared for. And that - effective and precise treatment - is what someone who wants to overcome the **art of being unhappy** should seek.

IS OUR MINDSET THE SAME AT HOME AS IT IS AT WORK?

Labor relations have changed a lot throughout history. From apprentices and masters of trades to modern *home workers,* the time, intensity, character and various characteristics of work have changed. But if there is one thing that remains unchanged, it is the fanciful understanding that work is work and personal life is personal life. In other words, there is a make-believe between bosses and employees that these two areas of life should not be mixed. The problem, however, is that life is one.

Let's think of a reverse situation: the person is bored at work and comes home in the evening upset and dejected. On the other hand, the spouse is very keen to have sex, but doesn't see reciprocity in their partner. What should you do? Put pressure on them to have sex or understand that the person who's upset at work has the same mindset as the one who can't bring himself to have sex?

Another situation. Try practicing a sport in which you are skilled when you have a serious concern on your mind... Imagine a soccer team, where there are 11 players on the pitch, all competent at what they do, but the positive results aren't coming. Surely the emotional state of some of them is compromised, but these things aren't brought up by the coaching staff, and even if they were, maybe the coach wouldn't know how to deal with them.

You have to understand that everything that happens in a person's life has repercussions between what happens in reality and in their imagination. Will a promotion at work lead you to celebrate with your family? Could a dismissal lead him to fall out with the same family? Similarly, could something good in the personal sphere, such as the birth of a child, make the person work better?

Notice that the sentences above are in interrogative form. It's a way of showing that even the birth of a child can help or hinder work. The child cries, the subject sleeps badly. A promotion can cause anguish, for fear that the person being promoted won't feel capable of the new task, disrupting family life. Resignation can bring relief and more satisfaction in family life, since the person might not be enjoying their job, although they wouldn't have the courage to resign.

Well, a person is one person, indivisible. Reading this, you probably thought: "How obvious!" True! However, in everyday life, where we spend most of our time - at work - this obviousness is constantly overlooked. It turns out that emotional aspects determine everything we do. The mind - or the imagination - feels and the body responds, no matter where we are, whether at home, at school, at college, at leisure or at work.

Our personality works in a similar way to computer *software*. How so? When we turn on the computer, the program always starts up the same way (for example, via Windows 7). When our mind is in action, thinking and feeling, it tends to work the same way. This mechanism was called repetition compulsion by Freud.

Why have I explained all this? To show that human beings carry this psychological baggage wherever they go and that there's no separating work from everything else. It's atavistic, it's intuitive, it's part of the race. And it's impossible to escape these dynamics. *C'est la vie*!

I think that a healthy institution that truly wants to engage with its employees would say the following: "Don't just bring your problems into the company, but here you will have the space to be heard!" Being heard doesn't mean that the company will solve the person's problem. You may think I've gone mad with this suggestion... But I invite some managers who are reading this text to reflect and perhaps try something different within their institution. If there was a space where employees could get together for half an hour a day and talk about their worries that day, it would be a therapeutic catharsis.

The human pretension of wanting to separate life into sectors is megalomaniacal. It's an attempt to control the uncontrollable, something that is very human. Whenever we're suffering from anguish or psychological discomfort, we get down on ourselves for the suffering itself and, what's worse, for not knowing the cause of this discomfort.

We also need to take into account the fact that we don't deal well or intimately with our psychic or emotional world. In this way, we become blind in one eye, i.e. we look at a person's life and performance from only one angle. This is how some bosses think: work is what matters, the rest is nonsense.

When we are faced with psychic suffering, a mechanism often used to try to protect ourselves is projection. Since we don't know the origin of the suffering, we tend to look outside ourselves for the explanation for the discomfort. It's easy to blame the external environment for the annoyance. Of course, we will always find an external cause to justify our theories, even if it doesn't make any sense. **This is how projection works: we look outside ourselves for an explanation.**

There are already companies that suggest that employees put faces or colors on panels where they work or even on their lab coats, selecting the image that best symbolizes their state of mind at that moment. That's nice, because you don't have to hide your emotions that day.

Institutions tend to think that mental and emotional suffering doesn't justify absence. They believe that only physical illness is a reason. Well, you should know that, depending on the case, it is possible to work with some physical pain, but with emotional pain it is difficult to do anything, because our thinking is paralyzed. Absenteeism at work can be a strong indicator of mental problems, such as depression and alcoholism.

In other words, it's worth paying attention to your employees. Look at their faces and see if they look upset or distressed. Even if they're happy, it's also healthy to try to find out why they're happy. If they're not doing their job properly, instead of telling them off, ask them if something is going on.

Does your company encourage employees to express their dissatisfaction with their manager without risking dismissal? Can they disagree with their manager? If so, your organization will have more engaged and healthier people at work.

VIAGRA AND COUPLES' SEX LIVES

Viagra is a well-known drug. It has been on the market for years and is intended to help men achieve erections during sexual intercourse. It's a wonderful advance, responsible for a great deal of satisfaction and well-being in the lives of many couples. However, there are some distortions that occur around the use of this medicine that are worth commenting on.

Men suffer from various forms of sexual difficulties. Lack of erection, partial erection, lack of desire, premature ejaculation, excessive delay in ejaculation. Our society is highly sexualized and much of the consistency of relationships between couples is based on sexual performance. However, this may not be enough. The body is used by both men and women as a lure, a bait so that the partner can be attracted and interested. This, of course, is inappropriate.

In this line of thinking, realize the importance of sexual performance to validate and consolidate the relationship. There is no such thing as female Viagra. Women are at a disadvantage because the pharmaceutical industry was initially concerned with catering for men, as they are the ones who run the world's big businesses. In other words, they run the finances and the economy.

Faced with this need to win over a partner via sex, male sexual potency is the number one, number two and perhaps number three priority! A man with impotence will become very depressed and will tend to withdraw from the female world. His esteem plummets. So how do you deal with such a problem? Erection difficulties are a constant - and huge - stumbling block for the male human being.

This is where the magic of Viagra comes in. Actually, it's not so magical, because it doesn't give everyone who uses it an erection. Luckily! Imagine if it worked in 100% of cases. Perhaps many men wouldn't think about winning over a woman with affection, affection, complicity, intimacy and love. Viagra would be enough!

However, I want to offer you a very particular view of sexual impotence, of *blowjobs*. I'm giving you my perception, which many people will not agree with *a priori*: I think it can be good if a man becomes impotent at the beginning of a relationship. I'm talking about a relationship that isn't ephemeral, fleeting; that isn't an "adventure", but something that can turn into a more intense relationship, with a bond and duration. I therefore defend the idea that it's not a bad thing for a man to occasionally *blow* a woman right at the beginning of his involvement with a woman with whom he intends to move on. And I explain my theory.

This unpleasant and embarrassing situation for a man can be a great opportunity for closer ties - all he has to do is talk to his partner about his difficult time. Please don't go out and use Viagra straight away! The vast majority of male sexual impotence, almost 100% of cases, is not usually associated with hormonal problems, such as a lack of testosterone. So there's no point in taking testosterone injections to improve your erection. Having said that, I can say that the main reason for impotence is of an emotional, *unconscious* origin.

We come back to the female role in the face of male impotence. I think that women cope very well with their partner's sexual difficulties at the beginning of the relationship. When the man talks truthfully about the anxiety that arises from that beginning, he brings the woman closer; she, in turn, will certainly feel part of the recovery of lost potency. They don't get frustrated or diminish their feelings for their partner because of erection difficulties. I see in the female universe that, when they meet a new partner, their priority is closeness, intimacy, getting to know each other, exchanging pleasantries and affection. Of course, they also want sexual fulfillment, but sex immediately seems to be part of the male universe, as if to mark territory *with a good "fuck"*.

Women are naturally welcoming and attentive. If they see that their partner is having a hard time, they'll take part in it and gladly help. And if men open the door to this, then they feel very valued. And this will strengthen the relationship. So instead of turning to a drug, men can turn to women.

So here's my theory: it's not a bad thing to eventually become impotent, as long as you're with a woman who is understanding, "competent" and for whom you have attraction, admiration and love. Viagra doesn't have to be ingested, it can be replaced with hugs, cuddles and feminine affection. Believe me, it usually works, even if it takes many days. Viagra can be by your side, in a skirt and lipstick, and it doesn't need to be bought in a pharmacy.

Attention, men, to these erectile difficulties. Don't go drinking to try to solve the problem. You'll become boring and aggressive - and the relationship will be at the mercy of the drink to make any sense. Alcohol increases sexual impotence, even if it makes you feel light and relaxed. Bad, isn't it?

* * *

Now, in older relationships, already solidified by time and complicity, Viagra can be a great ally. But it's important not to forget the values that have led the union through so many years of history - I'm talking about honesty, complicity and intimacy. I say this because it's common for men in long-term relationships to start taking Viagra, but to hide it from their partner. What would be the point of this kind of attitude, of camouflaging the fact that you're using Viagra? It could be evidence of a lack of intimacy, disrespect and inattention towards his partner.

Another possibility could be psychological. The guy wants to show himself to be the cool one, the bam-bam of the piece, the great one, which corresponds to wanting to show a reality that doesn't exist. Once again, some men feel that they are lesser, fragile and incompetent if they don't always have an erection. They fear that their partner will lose interest and look for other men. Evidently, these men who secretly use the medication are insecure, have little intimacy with an emotional relationship, little capacity to bond lovingly. The only power they imagine they have is sexual power, through erection.

Imagine this dissociation between the man who wants to have sex and uses Viagra in hiding, and the woman who isn't interested in sex that day.

Chaos! The guy with the erect penis, apparently showing great desire or arousal for the woman, but abandoned to his own devices. Or, worse, the woman submitting to his desire, even though she doesn't want to. There's a risk of creating distance between the couple.

It's healthier and more respectful to openly agree on the use of an additive for that festive moment. Don't forget to ask or feel in the exchange of caresses if your partner is willing or receptive to a sexual relationship at that moment.

BULLYING

Bullying is the conscious verbal abuse of a person or a group towards a person. It's the famous "making fun of", "making fun of", "picking on". For example: you meet a friend who used to be fat and who, after a diet, ended up losing weight. Instead of rejoicing with them, praising their efforts and celebrating their achievement, you say:

- Wow, what happened, did you catch AIDS to be thin like that?

Or you meet someone who was bald and has had a hair implant. Instead of commenting on the person's determination, or showing interest in the procedure, there's debauchery:

- Man, what is this! The most ridiculous thing to implant hair! It's not a man thing!

Her friend has gained weight and she makes a nasty comment:

- Is she pregnant? - even though I know she's not.

In other words, we tend to be dismissive, contemptuous and aggressively mocking. I'm talking about "you" and "we" here in a generic way, because it's something we see a lot in everyday life. These are manifestations of behavior that have always existed and are unlikely to cease to exist, something that is part of everyday human relations. But this can be reversed if we manage to watch our words and stop offending others gratuitously.

When we give someone a "nickname", we usually highlight aspects that diminish or disqualify them. Isn't that a form of *bullying*? Of course it is! I believe that the worst *bullying*, the most intense, frequent and striking is that which takes place within the home. Social *bullying*, in the sphere of work, sports, among friends, is perhaps better disguised because it has the mask of joking, of "making fun", of exercising freedom among friends.

At home, in the family, however, disqualification is more tolerated and with a degree of latent or explicit aggression. Parents who mistreat their children, devaluing their achievements and excessively criticizing their difficulties. Couples who criticize each other in all sorts of ways, bad-mouthing their partners or attacking their families of origin, which can go as far as shouting and swearing. Siblings who argue non-stop and try to hurt each other.

In short, there are many ways in which domestic *bullying* can manifest itself. Another form of *bullying* is the competition that parents encourage between their children, saying that one is better than the other. Here's another common occurrence. The child or teenager wants to give their opinion in a family conversation, which I think is very healthy. Parents or older siblings often say: "Shut up, don't get involved in this conversation, it's not for people your age!"

This approach is very damaging. It weakens relationships that should be intense, affectionate and encouraging. It generates discomfort and mistrust between people who should be accomplices and intimate. And in addition to these and other direct consequences, there are the emotional after-effects. A person brought up in a *bullying* family environment may find it difficult to defend themselves against this type of aggression when it arises in social or professional circles. They will be easy prey for the *bully*. On the other hand, in order to compensate for the passivity derived from the emotional anesthesia they have suffered throughout their life, they may develop an inordinate aggressiveness, directing it towards the more peaceful and calm people they live with. It's like the youngster who gets beaten up by the bullies at school and takes out his frustration on the weaker *nerds*.

I once went to the theater to see a *stand-up comedy*. This is a type of performance in which a comedian stands alone on stage, with only a microphone in hand, making jokes about common, everyday issues. This "show" I saw was built entirely around a kind of consensual *bullying*. All the actor did was mock, ridicule and even aggressively and rudely humiliate the people in the audience. In other words, everyone who was there, including myself, had paid for someone to mock them. Elderly people, women, people with aesthetic imperfections, men... No one escaped the comedian's professional debauchery.

A lady stood up and the comedian asked: "Are you going to pee? Is your bladder loose? Can't you wait until the show is over?" I left worried, because the laughter was running wild. It's clear that this show is a passing activity, where laughter dilutes the sadistic aspect of the artist; therefore, it won't make us sick. It's not *bullying* per se, which needs to be combated, but it is a way of diminishing others so that we can have fun. I mentioned this artistic activity more in the sense of thinking about the commonplace attitude of making fun of others. I confess that I left wondering if I wasn't the problem. Maybe I'm just too sensitive to these things!

But that's how this issue of *bullying* works: in a thousand disguises, in different forms, it is ingrained in all environments and in all human relationships - including those where there is genuine respect and appreciation.

One day, I was walking down the street with a friend who I know likes me very much. He has already told me in person how much he admires me and how much he enjoys my presence. On this occasion, however, we met some of his friends, to whom he introduced me:

- This is my friend Nélio Tombini. He's a psychiatrist, which means he's a bit crazy, so don't take too much notice of what he says.

You see, there's no doubt in my mind that this guy likes me. Even so, the way he introduced me was by denigrating me and making fun of me. I promptly used my best weapon, humor. I replied:

- Look, guys, I'm going to caption what he meant: he has great affection and admiration for me, but he finds it difficult to say so, perhaps because he thinks his integrity would be hurt. So he decided to show his affection for me by disqualifying me.

There was a laugh from the group.

I suggest that when faced with a *bullying* situation we should report it, speak clearly about our discomfort and tell the perpetrator. Tell your friend that he is disrespecting you; tell your family member that what he is doing is despising you; say that you didn't like a certain joke. Don't keep quiet. If you didn't have the courage or insight to take a stand at the time of the abuse, you can tell the abuser about your annoyance another day.

This behavior is very automatic, so we should be more attentive when we open our mouths to express what we think. I confess that I have said things that I later regretted. Whenever I could, I told the person that I had been rude, that I hadn't liked what I had said to them. I think this is a more appropriate way than just apologizing.

One of the dangers of people exposed to *bullying* in childhood is the possibility of them developing some kind of mental or psychological impairment over the course of their lives. They may become depressed, have low self-esteem, be irritable, complain, have some degree of social phobia or learning difficulties. What's worse is when these individuals also become abusers in the course of their own lives. An "eye for an eye, tooth for a tooth" reaction.

See how easy it is to develop the **art of being unhappy**! In the case of *bullying,* you try to make the other person unhappy. From a psychological point of view, the verbal attack, the disqualification of our interlocutor is an unconscious defense called projection. It means trying to transfer to the other person something that is ours - anxieties, annoyances, low self-esteem, insecurities and whatever else causes us discomfort. But it won't work, because our traumas need to be resolved by ourselves. There's no way of getting rid of them by judging or trying to transfer them to others.

It's very likely that seeing the other person down or upset gives us a false sense of satisfaction. In the collective unconscious, *bullying* can have the meaning of belittling others so that they don't belittle us. It's as if we were attacking, dumping our grudges on others before they do it to us.

Don't forget that the abuser's strategy, when faced with our annoyance at a disqualifying attitude, is to minimize what they've done by saying it was "just a joke". Of course, it's a bluff, because it makes no difference, since the damage is the same.

PSYCHOEDUCATION IN ORGANIZATIONS

What does psychoeducation mean? We are beings given to extremes when it comes to our feelings and emotions. And this characteristic is at the root of much of our suffering. It's no coincidence that, since Confucius and Aristotle, all the sages have pointed to the middle way - balance - as the route to possible well-being. I say this because, when we think of help for the ailments of the mind, people generally behave in two ways: either they shrug and don't bother at all, or they believe that they always need more intense treatment, such as an in-depth analysis.

If we are involved in emotional conflicts or want to get to know ourselves better, seeking individual psychotherapy is a good way to go. But we also have other possibilities for developing our ability to perceive emotions, to be more intimate with what we think and feel.

This book can be an alternative for transferring knowledge in the sphere of emotional life and, in this way, getting people to take a closer look at what they feel and how they react. The idea is that you, the reader, can also observe and perceive the other person's way of feeling and reacting. I call this process psychoeducation, or *coaching*.

From the point of view of physical health, we already know a lot. Think about the human body. We know how important it is to monitor weight, blood pressure, cholesterol, glucose, exercise, smoking and much more. We know about these problems and we can change them. Public bodies are running awareness campaigns, helping with prevention, which is very good.

As for emotional illness, nothing is done. Do you remember any advertising campaign - government or private - warning about the risks of emotional illness or anything like that? Emotional life is the compass of our lives, and yet it is denied, neglected, as if it were something second-rate. We think we can "handle" the difficulties associated with relationships, as if we were born equipped for these demands. Sad mistake!

When a person is paralyzed by depressive symptoms or anxiety, they feel that something is wrong. At that moment, they remember to go to a psychiatrist or psychologist. They will probably come out of it stronger. However, few people seek help from a mental health professional if they are not emotionally ill. The vast majority struggle and suffer on a daily basis, but think that this is life, that suffering is a natural part of life, and tend to look for a series of rational explanations to justify their malaise.

You can suffer too much in the face of your wife's refusal to have sex, an order from the boss, an invitation you didn't get (such as a trip with the company's board), your team's defeat, a politician's bullshit speech... We therefore need to be clear about the difference between not agreeing with something or getting upset and actually suffering, to the point of having some kind of psychic symptom.

The middle path between negligence and desperate concern is paved by knowledge, by self-education. This is the path I try to follow within companies and other professional and social organizations, with a method of instruction in which we talk about common issues, but which become immense difficulties if they are not clearly detected and tackled.

Through lectures, *workshops* and individualized or group talks, it is possible to shed light on fundamental concepts that are present and structured in our personalities and which, if not understood, can take over and undermine our personal and professional lives.

Let's talk about emotional or psychological *coaching*. *Coaching* is an English word that designates a personal training activity in which an instructor (*coach*) helps their client (*coachee*) to evolve in some area of their life. This isn't about giving "tips", but about equipping managers to be sensitive to and perceptive of the verbal, non-verbal, subliminal and unconscious messages that make up communication.

It's common to hear an employee classify the conduct or attitude of a company director or manager in relation to some employee demand as "stupid".

Dumb has to do with low intellectual capacity, low technical knowledge on a subject or low intelligence. In fact, in most situations, it's not a question of a lack of intelligence, because to be a director you need to have a good intellectual level. What we see in these people-related decisions is a lack of intimacy with emotional life.

Let's think of a common example from men's daily lives. A man who used to be sexually potent starts to become impotent. The likely course of action is to go to the urologist and want to take testosterone or Viagra, sure that it's a physical problem or a hormonal deficit. However, I can tell **you** that in 99.9% of cases the problem is in the head, in the emotional state of the person. If you insist on seeing a urologist, your impotence will only get worse. He'll need help from someone with the skills to deal with his emotional life.

The corporate world is no different. The tendency of directors or managers is to deal with others based on what their imagination suggests is most appropriate - which is not inappropriate. I see this behavior in goal planning. They plan in their heads: "We're going to achieve 20% growth this year", but they can't actually explain where they got the figure from or how they're going to get there. The challenge is set, and the employees have to work hard to achieve it. This behavior is related to grandiose, magical and omnipotent thinking, and does not relate to objective reality. Therefore, everything is bound to go wrong.

In other words, by talking about broad issues that are so common, we may be attacking problems that are hindering relationships and productivity in an organizational environment. Imagine the desire for control manifesting itself intensely in a boss. Or an employee who is unclear about the boundaries between power and power - between holding a position and having real authority over a matter. Or uncontrolled anger, the projection of personal difficulties onto others. In short. These are attitudes that seem trivial because they are so recurrent, but which are very damaging to the working environment.

Moral harassment has been increasingly highlighted within organizations. It seems to be a fever that has taken over the legal redress market. The most common thing today is for the labor courts to hear claims from people who are trying to earn some money by denouncing bullying. One reflection of bullying is the inability of managers to offer their employees their point of view with clarity, respect and politeness.

That's why it's very important for companies to think about looking for professionals with a keen eye for individual and collective psychic life, in order to facilitate relational processes. At a time when there is a constant concern about the physical health of employees, it's time to take care of the psyche too.

I often say - and I've said it in this book - that most people have a certain degree of **emotional illiteracy**. And it couldn't be any different: we have practically no clear and enlightening sources for seeking knowledge and information to help us in our own psychological education. The books that deal with these topics are usually very theoretical, dry and of little help to those who wish to expand their knowledge of the human psyche.

In the media, we receive countless guidelines on how to take care of our physical health, but we are completely abandoned when it comes to our minds, which are left in the background. This already demonstrates a deficiency that we face in both our individual and collective lives - and one that is growing in companies. Within institutions, complicity of ideas and attitudes is expected between those who guide actions and those who will carry them out. To achieve this, it is essential to be more familiar with the workings of the psychic apparatus.

Looking at another point, I invite you to think about the possibility of employees being able to express their state of mind or spirit when they arrive at work. It would be very interesting if, when we're not feeling well, we could share our problems with those around us, especially our bosses, without fear of prejudice or losing our jobs.

YOU'RE NOT THAT GOOD

We love to pretend that we are humble and modest. We invoke the formula "*modesty aside...*" to introduce a compliment we're going to give ourselves. The truth is that very often we say something that puts modesty to one side, so that it practically doesn't exist.

Some, however, tend to diminish themselves, thinking they have few values, not believing in themselves and failing to defend their points of view. Others, on the other hand, think they are much better than the rest, certain that they have a **lot on** their plate.

Certainly, the two situations described above are equally disruptive and will cause difficulties in these people's relationships.

It's good to support a point of view when we are convinced that it is appropriate and consistent. But even with the perception that we are right, I can tell you that one of the most recurring issues that annoys us on a daily basis is the unjustifiable need for others to agree with us. This issue of thinking we're special, of having a full head of steam, doesn't depend on how cultured, wealthy, educated, etc. we are. It has more to do with aspects of our personality than with external reality.

We then behave like inflexible ideologues: people who cling to an idea - in fact, a belief - and turn it into an ideology, wanting others to accept it. When we go down this road of believing we know everything, we stop talking to people. We start fighting real battles, which only end when the enemy falls, that is, when we break down the resistance of the interlocutor, who starts to agree with what we say. In the end, we begin to nurture and exercise the desire for control, to dominate the lives and thoughts of others, something like a dictator.

As great as the feeling of power generated by this behavior may be, know that it is a great source of suffering, conflicts, raids and even enmity - and a beautiful path to unhappiness. If you delve into this, you can be sure that people will only stay by your side out of fear, need or even interest. The others, who owe you nothing, will probably move away.

You may be a boss, manager or director in a company. Then your behavior will be swallowed up, at great expense, by your subordinates. However, they will take a great dislike to you. It's also possible that you'll be tolerated by one or other of your family members, one or other person with a close or affectionate bond (usually parents and children). Whenever someone submits to another, it soon evolves into a boycott, whether conscious or unconscious. In other words, the oppressed person ends up moving away or even making it difficult to carry out a task. In other words, there will always be a price to pay. Look around you. If this happens, it's very likely that you're behaving like someone who thinks they've got too much on their plate.

By doing so, you only harm yourself and others. Nothing good will come of it. Think about all the everyday situations you experience, not just the most direct relationships. If you think you're special, you can suffer a lot in ordinary situations, such as having to wait in line at the market or bank, a car overtaking you without signaling, an unanswered message from you, an appointment cancelled at short notice, etc.

Your gigantic ego will think: "Who am I to have to go through this?" Well, you're just an ordinary person, like everyone else. When you experience a major loss, whether material or in love, or the death of a loved one or a serious illness, you'll clearly understand what I'm talking about. We are all the same, and we are made equal by our fragility and finitude!

I've thought about being in charge of everyone, being welcomed and applauded by everyone, not being contradicted, being the owner of the truth and having *a very full ball.* But when I realize that my ball is sometimes a little shriveled and sometimes a little fuller, it does me good, because I'm confronted with reality - and I understand that I'm just one more being in this universe. My mind calms down and I become less demanding of myself.

No, we don't have all the power and morals that we sometimes think we do. In most cases, in almost all relationships and situations, each of us is just another person. It doesn't matter if you have a lot of money, if you have political influence, if you've published several books in your field, none of that. Without paying due attention to others, all you'll achieve are superficial relationships, maintained by the fear and need of those who are forced to relate to you. And that is definitely the pinnacle of the **art of being unhappy**.

Don't forget that human beings have a tendency to outsource their lives; in other words, they expect someone else to tell them what the best decision is or the best path to follow. This attitude encourages the action of a controller on duty or the guy who thinks he has the ball. We are surrounded by people like this. In my work, I see patients asking me what the solution is or the best way forward. I usually come away with this statement, which is true: "*How am I going to have a say in your life, if in some situations I don't even know what's best for me in my daily life?*". The role of a psychotherapist is to examine the possibilities with the patient, but not to decide for them the best way forward.

Nowadays, I like who I am more than I did a few years ago. Basically, I'm more aware of and better at dealing with my limitations, weaknesses and the impositions that life throws at me. I notice that I get less angry with the frustrations of everyday life. I think this is a good thermometer of emotional well-being.

I think that a good exercise in our daily lives is to pay attention to our reaction to our interlocutors, especially when they disagree with our explanations, requests, ideas or theses. If we tend to get angry in these so-called dialogues, it's a bad sign, because we want to beat our interlocutor and bring him or her to our truth. It's important to be attentive and focused on what's going on in our emotions, because we'll be able to see the difference in each person's way of expressing their thoughts. We'll probably be more tolerant of other people's so-called truths and move on to another topic, without feeling diminished or subjected by the other person.

The other day, I went to see a new restaurant that had been well recommended. When I got there, the owner stopped me when I tried to get in, saying that they were no longer serving meals. I asked what time it closed.

He replied and I realized that only five minutes had passed. I insisted, saying that it was only five minutes, but he was adamant, saying that he had this arrangement with his employees. I had the urge to get angry, but soon calmed down and left, accepting my frustration. If I had thought I had *too much* on my *plate*, I would have reacted with irritation and felt wronged. It was good for my heart and soul. I went elsewhere for lunch.

Perhaps what lurks in your unconscious, behind this high-flying, powerful boss behavior, is a feeling of intense fragility. If things don't go your way, your sense of powerlessness, of submission, rises up and takes over. Your emotions can't tolerate this experience and it pushes you to fight back. Control yourself. Breathe. Think. After all, neither you, nor I, nor anyone else has the ball...

DO YOU ALWAYS WANT TO BE RIGHT?

Do you realize how people want to impose their thoughts, their claims, their quibbles and be right? Many so-called dialogues are almost monologues, because they aim to arrive at a final, almost mathematical equation to find out who owns the truth. Conversation should be a way of venting, sharing our thoughts and being able to listen to the other person, even if we don't agree with their point of view. In everyday life, we see tyrants, even with great subtlety and polish, trying to impose their truths. The most literate, cultured and articulate person can, with great subtlety, be an *expert* in imposing their will.

The word *converse* comes from the Latin *conversare,* which originally meant to live with someone, to be intimate, to be close. Today, conversation can have the weight of a fight, to see who wins, comes out the victor, kills the other. It seems that, for some, the risk of conversation is to push the other away, instead of bringing them closer, welcoming them, even when they disagree.

We want to be valued, welcomed and applauded by those around us. This tension can cause problems and suffering for a large number of people. In what way? Through disagreements, conflicts and the intransigence with which we react to life's contingencies. We have many beliefs that are preconceived ideas and are ingrained in our minds, and we carry these thoughts into everything we do in life.

We live in constant conflict. We can't live without them, which sometimes occur with the external world (others) and sometimes with the internal world (ourselves). In this text, I'll focus on external clashes with our surroundings.

We have the so-called objective conflicts of everyday life, inherent to life, which involve conversations between the parties to resolve them: deadlocks in the renting of a property; an unfulfilled agreement; an undue charge; a difficulty in traffic; an unconfirmed arrangement; a task done differently from what was agreed; a break-up in love; arguments over political, religious or cultural ideologies; and endless other reasons.

When we're in a conflict, in a debate, discussing ideas, projects, abstract or concrete things? It doesn't matter - where there's a dispute, someone wants to impose their opinion. This is yet another natural tendency of this strange human being: to always want to be right. "My word must be last".

It goes without saying that we have to use all our reasoning and argumentation, because it's important in everyday discussions that our point of view is taken into account. But my question is precisely this:

In some situations, what would be the difference between agreeing or disagreeing with our argument, with our considerations?

It seems that, for insecure people, the possibility that someone doesn't think like them brings with it a feeling of submission, disqualification, belittlement, as if they had lost a fight. Being left without reason, without being heard, can be felt by some to be the same as knowing that they have no value. Continuously, irritation and anger can manifest themselves as defense mechanisms. For those who hold themselves in higher esteem, they will certainly see these experiences as natural occurrences, less painful.

In my life, I've been through countless situations in which I've felt wronged - in other words, times when I thought I was right, but I didn't get what I wanted. I remember how much energy I spent, inside myself, brooding, rethinking, fighting in my mind with someone who didn't agree with my thoughts. Of course, I never came to blows because they didn't accept my arguments.

Let me give you an example. A bank sent me a credit card that I hadn't applied for. I wasn't even a customer of the bank. In fact, the card never even reached me. However, after a while, I started being charged for the card's annual fee without having received it. I contacted the people responsible, to no avail. After a while, a law firm started calling me every day, as if it were torture, to get me to pay the debt. Behold: the amount was 65 reais. I thought about paying to get rid of it, but I thought I'd be an accomplice to this scam. I called the office and explained everything, but it didn't work. I was only able to resolve it when I went to court, to the small claims court. I didn't receive any compensation for moral damages, but they stopped giving me hell. Of course, I suffered a lot, but I realized that I hadn't managed to convey my reasons to them, so to reduce my level of irritation, I went to court. I wish they had taken more notice of me. Once again, I realized how insignificant I was in life. I wanted to be accepted for my reasons, but to no avail.

That was one situation, but there would be many others to show how important it is not to let ourselves be emotionally overwhelmed by cases in which, despite having all the reasons in the world, we end up having to give them up and look for an alternative way out.

In discussions between couples, I see how difficult it is to live together when one spouse thinks differently from the other about everyday matters. They may go so far as to rethink whether it's worth staying married to someone who thinks completely differently. Look at all the tyrants and dictators on duty out there!

Along these lines of the masters of reason, pay attention to the way some individuals pretend to engage in dialog. They appear to be listening to their interlocutor, but in fact they're just waiting for an opportunity to get back to them with their ideas. They don't bother to listen to the other person's thoughts, because they see themselves as the masters of reason and want to impose their thoughts. Politicians are *experts* at this. If you notice this type of person in a conversation, I think it's a good idea to make it clear to them how you relate to them.

At Psicobreve, the clinic for which I am responsible, I have seen patients who were late and missed their appointment. Faced with this unpleasant fact, some of them would "come up with reasons", making lame excuses and creating conflictual situations with the receptionists, wanting to be attended to in any way they could. I even interfered on one occasion, showing the person that they were already really upset about missing their appointment and that being full of reasons wouldn't change the course of things, it would just make them more upset and angry.

I remembered an episode with a friend and his teenage son. In some situations, the son didn't fulfill some task agreed upon or expected by his father. Faced with clear reasons and paternal considerations, the son wouldn't change his mind or his attitude. It became a challenging relationship with risks of loss of control for both. The father got angry, wanted to fight, but thought: "What to do? Disqualify him, force him to do the task or go on endlessly, to see if he changes his mind?"

I suggested that he interrupt the discussion when an impasse arose with the risk of losing control of the parties, that he try to resume the subject a few days later, without the weight of the strong emotion of that previous discussion. He would give up his conviction of reason in order to turn it into an effective and - at times - efficient conversation. It's a way of giving up being right in order to reach the desired point, through reflection, confrontation and argumentation.

The big problem is that, more often than not, those who want to discuss everything with everyone are not really interested in the subject of the discussion, in the fact that is on the agenda. All they want is a space and an audience to say what they think, to show off. Proof of this is that this person will almost always counter your opinion about something with a personal criticism. You say what you think about the current economic policy, for example, and the subject, instead of countering your opinion on the issue, disqualifies you with some offense against your characteristics. This is a rhetorical resource called *argumentum ad hominem* - in other words, an argument aimed not at what is being discussed, but at the person who is discussing it.

It's worth describing a little more this frequent attitude of disqualifying one's interlocutor in debates, with the intention of coming out on *top*. It's a clever way of trying to put the other person down, because it often attacks the other person's moral conduct, even if there's no real basis for it. The strategy goes something like this: "If I don't win by talking, I'll win by shouting." And that can actually work.

Good examples of this can be found in discussions about politics. In the Brazilian context, one person calls another "coxinha" or "mortadela". If the person is offended by the nickname, they lose the ability to reason and give power to the other. That's how we are, we want to beat anyone who opposes our reasons or beliefs.

Indeed, what is the point of these people always wanting to be right? Behind this behavior lie some psychological mechanisms that may justify this pattern of conduct. One of them is the desire for control, the desire to be in charge and lead other people - a mechanism I talk about a lot in this book. Little children are already bossy, they want to control everything and everyone by crying, refusing to eat, etc.

Also hidden in these struggles for reason is another feeling, that of insecurity or inferiority. If they are unable to impose their reason, they are invaded by a feeling of worthlessness, as if they were being subjected to others. The next step in trying to get rid of these bad feelings is uncontrollable anger, which can lead to aggression.

It should be clear that, at one time or another, we are all possessed by these feelings - it's human. A good indicator of whether we've done well in such an argument is to see how angry we are afterwards. If you're not very angry, that's a good sign. If you're very angry, watch out, because it's very likely that you think you've been defeated or that you've submitted to the other person.

CAN MENTAL ILLNESS GIVE YOU POWER?

Silvia is 30 years old, single, university educated, intelligent, competent and capable. She lives with her parents and is not working at the moment. Her parents had planned a trip to Europe and flew to São Paulo, where they were waiting for their connection abroad. Sílvia then telephoned her parents to tell them that she was very anxious and unwell about staying at home on her own. She feared she would go mad or die of a heart attack if they didn't return.

To the girl's disgrace, her parents ended up moving back to Porto Alegre, leaving their plans aside. Yes, it was not only her parents' misfortune, who left their plans aside. It was just as bad for the young woman, as she received positive reinforcement for maintaining her illness. It's as if she received a bonus, reinforcing the idea that she was fragile, and only the presence of her parents could calm her down. Her parents, on the other hand, thought they were very important in her life, so they were not far from her. For a long time, they had given her unusual care, to the detriment of their other children.

She lost her job as a result of the damage caused by her illness. She was afraid of being alone, of going out unaccompanied, she hoarded objects and feared catching diseases (which meant she had to wash her hands a lot). At home and in the company of her parents, she felt full, safe and free of anxieties.

This story sounds like that of superheroes who, called up in a hurry, show up to save someone. Or was Silvia the hero, able to control and change her parents' path with one move? Well, that's a true story. In fact, her apparent superpowers serve to cover up her psychological or emotional fragility. This is a girl who is frightened and insecure about her life.

We can clearly see the harmony that occurs between uncomfortable psychiatric symptoms and the patient's daily life. Of course, it's not a conscious set-up by the patient to take advantage of her symptoms; it's something produced unconsciously in her imagination. In fact, he doesn't benefit, but loses out in his process of individualization, development and growth. It seems crazy, pointless, surreal. But for our unconscious or imaginary, nothing is surreal, everything is possible, everything is absolutely understandable.

This experience shows a subliminal family collusion, because the parents also needed their adult daughter to stick to them. Something like this: "You only grow in age, but emotionally you remain an insecure, dependent child who clings to us." This symbiosis also points towards a gain for the parents in the future - something like this: "We look after you like a child and, when we get older, you'll look after us." Through these symptoms, he developed a style of relating to his parents in which his psychiatric illness empowered him. You see, a person with mental problems can turn their suffering into "power".

For this equation to work, there is a need to develop this type of emotional illness. This is how our unconscious creates traps capable of diverting healthy development and creating a breeding ground for the **art of being unhappy**.

It's hard for people to get out of it on their own, because they have no idea what's going on, how they fell into this trap. Psychotherapy is one way to get them out of this trap. Medication can reduce anxiety, but it won't really solve it or get to the heart of the problem, which is not chemical but psychological. Family psychotherapy would also be an interesting alternative.

Today, Silvia is much better. Her symptoms have decreased dramatically. She is able to realize that she used her problems to sabotage herself in the first place - and to control the people around her, especially her parents. She can make fun and jokes about what she went through and how she acted. She has traveled alone. And her parents have already managed to go to Europe.

* * *

I also remember a 15-year-old boy who lived with his mother because his father, who was separated, lived in another state. The son wanted to live with his father, but his mother wouldn't accept it. The young man became depressed and began to mutilate himself, cutting his arm and forearm with a blade. The mother became frightened, fearing that her son would kill himself. The mother wanted to know what to do, because she feared her son would commit suicide and was thinking of having him committed to a psychiatric clinic. That's why she came to me.

When I spoke to the young man, I didn't see any risk of suicide, but a desire to force his mother to give in to his desires. He was trying to use his mental suffering to gain an advantage over his mother. There was a power struggle, with the mother on one side and the son on the other. Of course, there was a risk of hospitalization, but that would only increase the son's frustration and anger. The therapeutic intervention helped both of them to develop a healthier, clearer and more objective ability to communicate. Verbal expression took the place of mutilating attitudes. In other words, power came through the clear word of wanting to be with the father. The mother acquiesced.

* * *

I hope, through these examples, I've managed to show you how mental illness can generate "power" in those who present themselves as ill - but a harmful power that only weakens.

WHY DO WE CARRY SO MUCH GUILT?

Let's talk about a great human invention. An invention that changes lives and determines destinies, leading people, couples and even entire families towards permanent suffering. I'm talking about the **feeling of guilt**. It's so old among us that its origin cannot be determined. This habit of ours seems to be a characteristic of our essence, something we were born with. But the truth is that it is something that has been built up, in a civilizational and religious way.

This invention comes from the same source that permeates Western civilization. I'm talking about Judeo-Christian morality. This morality was formed on the basis of beliefs that the creator, God, was someone who was very strict, demanding and imposed his will. God, in fact, is merciful and exempts from guilt those who repent of their mistakes or sins, but regardless of this, the feeling of guilt is already embedded enough in the *ethos* (the way of being, the character, the ethical values and habits) of this civilization.

Religious issues aside, whether you're a believer or a skeptic, the fact is that in everyday life it's hard to escape this feeling of guilt - unpleasant and sometimes paralyzing. I'll share with you some of the manifestations I've heard. Things like:

"I'm to blame for my son taking drugs. I made a mistake in his upbringing and that's why he's lost his way in life..."

"My wife left me because of me. I could have acted differently and prevented the separation..."

"We were fighting when my father died. It was all my fault! Did I kill him out of grief?"

"I don't care about women anymore. I blame my fiancée because she ruined my life, she left me..."

"Where did I go wrong?"

And so on.

First of all, it has to be said that, yes, we could always have acted differently, for better or for worse. We could have, but we didn't at the time. We did what we could have done. Life is like that. We act according to our impulses, projects, reflections, apparent certainties and according to the contingencies that present themselves. The Spanish philosopher Ortega y Gasset defined the **self** perfectly: "*I am me and my circumstances.*" In other words, we are what we are, but we are constantly adapting to everything that happens to us.

Without a shadow of a doubt, the worst guilt we can bear doesn't come from God, but from within ourselves. Unconsciously, the guilty person perpetuates this suffering, as if they needed to punish themselves. Out of a masochistic desire to solidify this feeling, they look outside themselves for the source of their suffering, finding culprits and evildoers to justify the reason for their disorder. Of course, it's not at all difficult to find culprits in our surroundings. This is how this unease becomes entrenched, which would seemingly remain unresolved and repeat itself forever. To assuage the feeling of guilt, the subject then develops a ritual of penalization, penance and purgation to try to rid themselves of this evil. Of course, there will be no solution through this path.

Following this line of thought, in which the feeling of guilt is a production of the individual and not of God, I will describe two structures that are present in people's imaginations, to a greater or lesser extent. I'm talking about the feeling of grandiosity and omnipotence. These two mechanisms are similar and often go hand in hand. They create an idea in people's minds that they are very powerful, the masters of the truth. They allow themselves to meddle in everything; they know what's good for others and think they can solve everything. He gets angry, contradicting himself. God may be omnipotent, omnipresent and omniscient, but we are fragile and mortal beings? That's too much!

Within this individual who imagines himself to be so powerful, the perfect breeding ground develops for the proliferation of feelings of guilt and, consequently, for the individual to experience that he is the cause of all misfortunes. It's egolatry. Me, me, me. Go back to the examples I gave of people who blame themselves and notice that the word "I" recurs a lot.

It may seem paradoxical; after all, someone who blames themselves a lot would appear to be down, down, down. However, if the person is putting the result of all their failures on their own shoulders, it's because they think they have enormous power, always able to change the course of events; therefore, they place themselves on high, better and more capable than everyone else. Hold on! We don't have all that.

I remember a girl who had a terrible sense of guilt, with damaging consequences for her daily life. She accidentally became pregnant and had thoughts of abortion. She didn't do it and is very happy with her child, but she continues to purge, suffer and live a wandering life, just because she thought about killing her own child. Thinking bad thoughts, of course, is not a sin and doesn't land anyone in jail. In this case, the person thinks they are very important, great, just because they thought it.

What the human being, this fragile little being, can have at most is responsibility towards life, for his actions. That's all, much less than the feeling of guilt, which is for those who think they have too much on their plate. Of course, every time I make a decision, I can cause annoyance, suffering, upset, damage - to myself and to others. That's life. It's as simple as that.

It is necessary to have a sense of responsibility. To take care of what is yours, what is in your charge; but always aware of your limits and the limits of the situation. We are responsible for the decisions we make, but we don't know what will happen after a decision is made or a word is said.

Whenever I hear someone making choices between a supposed right and a supposed wrong, I confess that a red light goes on inside my head. The simplistic idea that everything can be summed up as right or wrong shows that the person who carries this structure of thought is someone who has absolute truths in their mind, attuned to grandeur and omnipotence and fertile ground for developing the ill-fated feeling of guilt.

* * *

More than 20 years ago, my mother was in Porto Alegre, in hospital with her second husband, who was in a coma as a result of terminal cancer. I noticed that she was tired and down. So I insisted that she go to the beach for the weekend with my sister, who was there. I would watch my stepfather. My mother, at 70, was a very active woman, driving and getting around without any difficulty. She was unsure about going, but I insisted. She went. On the way, she had an accident and died.

I confess to you, reader, that I was very sad, upset and down. But I didn't let the feeling of guilt take over. If I had, my life would have become a great tragedy. She went to the beach by her own decision, even though I encouraged her to do so. As far as we know, she got into an accident because she was careless and reckless. What happened was simply a fatality. Sad, regrettable, but with no one actively to blame. Of course, all this didn't take away the pain of having lost her like that.

PREJUDICE AGAINST MENTAL ILLNESS

The World Health Organization predicts that by 2025 depression will be the second most common disease in the world population, second only to cardiovascular diseases. This statistical projection does not include other psychiatric illnesses that are constantly on the rise, such as alcoholism, addiction to cocaine, marijuana and *crack*, attention deficit hyperactivity disorder, anxiety syndromes (panic, *burnout*, stress, phobias, obsessive compulsive disorder) and bipolar disorder.

I want to emphasize that when I refer to psychiatric or mental problems that give rise to prejudice, I am not referring to psychotic people, people in a state of madness, people who have lost their critical judgment.

People talk calmly about the ailments of the body, listen attentively, give advice, talk about medicines, teas; in other words, they take an interest and try to help those who are physically ill. Public health bodies inform the population on radio and TV about campaigns to treat or prevent physical illness. At the time of writing, there is a campaign to combat yellow fever, another for Zika, yet another for dengue, obesity, etc.

Do you remember any government advertising campaigns focused on mental illness? I bet you don't! Why is there no concern about the psychiatric problems that incapacitate so many people, so many families, causing huge losses for the government as a result of time off work? There is no concern because the mentally ill suffer in silence, isolate themselves, claim nothing, feel like outcasts of society, useless. They don't claim anything and little is offered to them by public bodies. What's worse: the family itself can't tolerate living with the mentally ill person.

Have you ever seen someone making fun of or mocking a hypertensive patient, a diabetic, someone with a gluten intolerance or a cancer patient? No, right?

The psychiatric problem is already too heavy a burden to carry. The patient himself is prejudiced against himself. In addition, the person has to deal with various misunderstandings, prejudice and mockery. I've already said in this book: physical illnesses are taken seriously, while mental illnesses are neglected, seen as *frills* or personal failures.

- You're crazy!

That's what you hear most often. In other words, it's despised, it becomes a joke. And it gets worse when it comes to someone who is trying to understand and resolve their suffering, their internal conflicts - conflicts, by the way, that we all have, to a greater or lesser degree. I've heard several patients complain that, in any argument, in any raid, their relatives say:

- You're crazy. You can't take someone who goes to the psychiatrist and takes medication seriously.

These disqualifications also occur among friends, in love relationships and at work.

You don't expect someone to arrive at work and tell a colleague or boss that they're depressed, or very anxious, afraid to walk alone in the street, that they feel short of breath when they get into the elevator, that they don't have the energy to do their job? Why don't we usually share this kind of suffering with others? I answer: because of prejudice, fear of being laughed at, or because the other person has no interest in hearing this kind of talk. It seems that these subjects are contagious.

Imagine yourself being interviewed for a job while you are being treated for depression or insomnia. Would you say that you're under psychiatric supervision, taking antidepressants? Of course not, because then the chance of not getting the job would be 101%. On the other hand, there's a good chance that the job will help you overcome your depression. Depression, if treated, can improve and is not a burden on you for the rest of your life, so it is possible to regain your working power. (On the other hand, if you take medication for high blood pressure or cholesterol, you wouldn't be embarrassed or afraid to mention this in an interview for a job...)

Realize the harsh reality that people with psychiatric problems live with. Pure prejudice. The other day I was approached by a couple from a low economic background who wanted to adopt a child, even a child born with a treatable illness. They underwent a psychological assessment with the judiciary's social services and were barred because the lady had a diagnosis of bipolar disorder and had been admitted to a psychiatric hospital in the past.

When I talked to the couple, but more attentively to her, I noticed vigorous mental health, adequate affection, preserved critical judgment and no signs of mental illness. If I hadn't known about her illness, I wouldn't have noticed any signs of bipolar disorder at that meeting; therefore, her illness was under control. She was adequately medicated for bipolar disorder. She did activities at home to help with the couple's income. She was hospitalized because at the time of the crisis she didn't know she was ill. I issued a report in favor of adoption, because this treated person is capable of taking charge of her life and also of a child. I'm not irresponsible, but in this case I saw pure prejudice against a person because of the label of bipolar disorder.

Now we have to ask ourselves:

Why do people disqualify those who suffer from emotional or psychiatric illnesses?

I understand that this happens as a form of defense, a pseudo-protection. By attacking and despising the other person, they think they are keeping away the possibility that they themselves might suffer from a mental illness at some point. What would go through the prejudiced person's unconscious would be something like this: "Far be it from me, these crazy, weak, weak-willed people who have no shame in their faces!"

They place themselves on a different level, as if they were completely different human beings. The critic would be the healthy one, belonging to a privileged caste. The other, the sick person, would belong to a lower caste. Of course, this is a defense against something that is feared in the imagination. Of being emotionally ill too. No one is free from facing psychological and psychiatric problems at some point in their life.

Prejudices are so intense that society has created a division between psychiatrists and psychologists. The former treat people who are sick or crazy and give them medication. Psychologists treat healthier people, as they only talk to them and don't give them medication. To clarify, psychiatrists, as well as being able to prescribe medication, also carry out psychotherapy. Psychologists are only qualified to do psychotherapy. Both professionals help people recover their mental health.

I'd like to remind you that 40% of the population uses some form of psychiatric medication. Didn't you know that? Rivotril, a black-belt tranquilizer, is one of the best-selling drugs in Brazil.

Look at yourselves, at the people you live with, and realize how many suffer from some emotional problem, leading to a greater or lesser degree of disability. How many people in your family or social circle have problems with alcohol? Marijuana use? Excessive irritation or aggression? Insomnia? Anxiety or panic symptoms? Sexual difficulties of a psychological nature? The presence of psychiatric symptoms or even mental illnesses is more prevalent in the general population than physical illnesses linked to the body.

So let's be more generous with people suffering from mental illness, of greater or lesser intensity. In many cases, they think they are "garbage", second-class people. Let's not put them down. It's not healthy to throw stones at other people's roofs when your own is made of glass. This is my analogy for those who are prejudiced against mental illness. It would be a good way to take the intensity out of the art of being unhappy in our daily lives.

WHAT STRONG PERSONALITY MEANS

The term **personality** comes from the Latin word *persona,* which means mask - but not in the sense of a shield to hide our face. Personality - or character - is the set of psychological characteristics that determine patterns of thinking, feeling and acting. Freud compared a healthier personality to shades of color. The more the individual's personality adapted to the context, the healthier he or she would be; in other words, color would be better than one or two colors. Personality is almost an individual's fingerprint, as it is unique to each person and cannot be repeated in another, even in univitelline twins.

Here's something we hear a lot: "That guy has a strong personality." Its connotation even suggests a compliment, as it is usually said to people who are firm, have solid convictions and an unflappable demeanor. However, it is an expression that is as overused as it is meaningless. And it is only valid if taken as a mere expression, as a figure of speech to describe someone whose positions are well defined, with a marked demeanor.

The truth is that saying someone has a strong personality is a euphemism we use to define a person who tends towards intransigence, whose stance is imposing and inflexible. This is the person who gets angry if things don't go their way, who has no qualms about expressing their indignation when someone displeases them, who thinks they know what's good for others and always has an opinion on any subject. If they're upset, they tend to get angry, shout at others, bully them and mistreat them.

From a scientific point of view, there is no concept of personality type. It's more of a popular convention. But in the light of everyday life, it seems that it's good to live with or be around this type of person, as if they were looking after us and taking charge of our lives. When it's said that the person with the *strong personality* acted "this way or that way", even if they have a stance that hurts or is inappropriate towards the other person, there's no shortage of people who justify the inappropriate behavior by saying: "*Oh, but he has a strong personality...*" It sounds like an alibi for some people who are truculent with words.

And who is the preferred target of the supposedly strong personality? Who suffers most from that intransigent, imposing person? I'm allowing myself to create a neologism, a new type of personality, to try to answer the above questions. The person who suffers most would be the person with, let's say, a **weak personality** - something that doesn't really exist from a psychiatric point of view either. I'm talking about the person who lowers their head to anyone, who submits, is passive, doesn't decide anything and waits for others to lead them through life. *Read the article "Let life take me...", which is in this book, and learn more about the main victim of those who boast a supposedly strong personality.*

One detail: this person with the supposedly weak personality isn't really that weak. Why? I make this distinction because it's important to note that, in the end, both personalities - the strong and the weak - want the same thing: control of the environment, the situation, the people. In the "strong" one, this is quite evident, because his posture and procedures are loud, showy.

In the "weak" person, this is more hidden, disguised. Perhaps the "weak" person doesn't realize it, but their passive attitude, their posture of always waiting for others, is also a form of domination. This is because they don't do anything, they don't decide, they aren't clear, but they give clues and lead others to take responsibility for the decision, but in the end, they do what they want. There is a popular gaucho saying that there are clever people who "play dead to get new shoes". This would be the weak personality, who takes advantage of supposed weaknesses to gain an advantage.

At the end of the day, both the supposed strong personality and the supposed weak personality are quite different disguises for villains with very similar pretensions, which can be summed up as controlling situations, people and environments. These are self-centered individuals. They need special attention, which they demand in different ways - one by shouting, the other by silence.

They're like children. Most babies draw attention to themselves by crying, which is very natural and essential for survival. As they grow up, they change their attitude patterns to get what they want. However, some children return to the practice of crying - which easily turns into tantrums and "ranhentice" - in order to dominate their parents; others, on the other hand, are the difficult type, shutting themselves in, keeping quiet, not eating or playing. Despite their very different behaviors, both types of child want the same thing: all the attention in the house. And they demand it through the famous "antics".

* * *

A synonym used to describe the strong personality type is "ornery". This is someone who is irascible, sour or irritable. *Genious* comes from *genius,* which in Arab folklore designates evil characters, who can take on various shapes and sizes, appearing in male and female versions.

The legend of *Aladdin and the Magic Lamp* does not exist in *The Thousand and One Nights.* The tale first appeared in a French version of the book by Antonie Galland at the beginning of the 18th century. In the tales of *The Thousand and One Nights* published outside the Arab world, only Aladdin's genie *and* the *genie of* the first tale, *The Fisherman and the Genie,* are imprisoned and grant wishes. It would be a Western version creating the genies of good.

* * *

The aim of this text is not to disqualify people with these characteristics, but rather to shed a little light on the universe of our psychic functioning and, in this way, become more intimate with it. Look around you, or at yourself, and see if there isn't an adult out there with these traits - whether they're shouty or quiet, with a "strong" or "weak" personality. Don't forget that it's not healthy to embody either of the two personalities described in the text.

PSYCHOTHERAPY MAY BE THE SOLUTION

Imagine two pillars giving support and harmony to our lives, our relationships and our well-being. One of the pillars is linked to our knowledge, culture, learning, intelligence - in other words, intellectual and cognitive aspects. The other pillar has to do with our emotional, sentimental or psychic life - with our unconscious.

We have more access and can develop and take better care of the first pillar, the one linked to knowledge. Why is that? Because, if we have the interest and time, we can study, work, dedicate ourselves diligently and achieve a good intellectual performance, learn a new language, do an MBA, pass a competitive exam, etc. However, the pillar linked to the emotional is more complicated and difficult to control and access; nevertheless, it exerts supremacy and has an enormous influence on our daily lives. It has great influence and determines the success and performance of the intellectual pillar. However, the reverse is not true: the intellectual does not influence the emotional as much.

Why did I make this analogy with the pillars? So that you know that the psyche - or emotional - is the balance; in other words, our ability to have a more satisfying, successful and pleasurable life passes through the filter and sieve of the emotional. Just being intelligent, studious and having money may not help much if we don't have the partnership of the blessed - or cursed - emotional.

A few years ago, I read a survey of executives from large companies in the national Você S/A magazine. They were asked what an important, unconventional, alternative investment would be to differentiate themselves in their job. Behold: 60% said that psychotherapy or analysis would be a good alternative. (For the sake of simplicity, I'll use psychotherapy and psychoanalysis as synonyms here).

But what is psychotherapy?

I've heard this question many times and I realize that there is a very vague idea about this method of treatment. In a nutshell, psychotherapy is a process of transference, through words, of perceptions between a therapist (psychiatrist or psychologist) and a patient. The patient puts their, shall we say, emotional issues on the table for the therapist, who will try to unravel what is at the bottom of it, in the subterranean of the mind, trying to disarm the unconscious traps. The patient may be anxious or depressed, without knowing the origin of these symptoms. The psychotherapist, listening to their story, will try to clarify the unconscious source of these sufferings. And the person, in contact with these insights, will be able to improve.

And what is the unconscious?

It's a reservoir of repressed impulses, as if they were emotions that exist inside us and are trying to surface. For example, a child whose father used to raise his voice (threatening him and making him nervous) may grow up with these emotions hidden in his mind. In adulthood, simply hearing the boss speak in a more intense tone of voice will make her anxious, to the point of crying, even though she knows she's not being cursed at or threatened. This reaction may come from the unconscious, where repressed emotions have remained. Our dreams and failed acts are also clear examples of the presence of the unconscious.

* * *

We can make a correlation between the unconscious and knowledge of a language. Imagine a person in a strange country where they don't understand the local language. This would generate a lot of anxiety and nervousness, perhaps leaving the person paralyzed. But if a translator came along and told them what those words meant, there would be great relief.

Psychotherapy therefore serves to unlock the patient, to get them out of a zone of suffering in which they are sinking deeper and deeper. The therapist's task, therefore, is to listen to the patient's stories and offer explanations and alternatives to the suffering they are experiencing. Don't confuse this with giving advice. Friends are good enough to give us advice.

I'll give you an example of a case I came across: a man who lost his mother to a heart attack at a time in his life when they were fighting a lot. After a few months, he began to show symptoms that suggested he had heart problems - chest discomfort, pain and shortness of breath. He then went to different doctors and emergency services, who were unanimous in telling him that he didn't have any heart problems.

This man's case was one of unresolved grief. His body was showing signs of the trauma of losing his mother, of seeing her go without being able to say goodbye as he would have liked. There was a strong sense of guilt. Listening to him for a short time was enough to realize that his problem wasn't in his physical heart, but in his metaphorical heart - in his soul, in his imagination. But perception is only part of the process. The next challenge is to communicate to the patient what you have been able to understand about their problems. If you manage to make them understand this perception, you generally have resolved an emotional hang-up, disarmed a trap of the mind.

Another example: an executive who always traveled by plane for work and pleasure began to develop an anxiety, almost panic, about going on vacation with his wife. It would be a longer vacation, the first time he would go abroad with his wife. What was different in this case was that, although he already traveled without any problems, he began to feel afraid. In conversations with me, we realized that there was a conflict in the depths of his psyche, which could explain the emergence of these recent fears of flying.

He had always been very attached to his widowed mother, but after he got married, he became more distant from her. His mother started putting pressure on him, demanding and showing some resentment. She said that she had given up her things to give him everything, studies, clothes, etc., and that he was going to have fun with his wife and wasn't thinking of taking her with him. He didn't really want to take her, but he didn't have the courage to talk about it clearly. The mother, for her part, played the victim, the poor, abandoned girl, so that her son wouldn't leave her. And the worst thing for her was that her son would travel with his wife and not take her. A double betrayal!

This man simply couldn't tell his mother what to say. So, since he couldn't verbalize a response to his mother, he ended up punishing himself and boycotting his trip. The presence of the fears of traveling would help resolve the situation. In doing so, she believed she would be free of the problem - since she wouldn't leave her mother alone and wouldn't have to face her drama. And it is precisely here that a psychotherapist fits like a glove, with his task of identifying the problem and pointing out a way to get rid of it once and for all.

This is all very important because our emotional issues determine the whole of our lives. How we feel, how we interpret what we hear, how we see the world, how we see ourselves and how we relate to others determine a large part of the quality of our lives. And the rest of that quality - from work, friendships, love and family ties, for example - depends on factors determined directly by our emotional conditions. This is why psychotherapy can be so important: because it can help you perceive subliminal conflicts and solve problems that can unlock your life.

The search for help in my area of work is based on a great deal of prejudice that people have towards mental suffering. We look at people who go to a psychiatrist as if they were weak, fragile or even crazy. Prejudice is directly related to our ignorance. When we don't know how to explain or understand a feeling we have, we tend to see it as something we disqualify.

Psychotherapeutic approaches are not only suitable for individuals, but are also useful for families, couples, groups of patients and business organizations. So-called psychotherapeutic interventions have brought promising results in organizations, working with managers and teams. These activities are one-off and can be repeated from time to time. It is a way of enabling professionals to deal more competently with their employees, as they are able to perceive and understand unconscious behaviors and messages.

THOSE WHO OFFER THEMSELVES WILL BE MORE SUCCESSFUL

"Come on, let's go / waiting is not knowing / those who know make the time / don't wait for it to happen..."

As simple as they are beautiful and ingenious, the verses of a song by Geraldo Vandré, written at the time of the military regime, perfectly sum up what I mean by this text. **Offer yourself.** Don't hide. Show yourself, present yourself. Those who know make the time, don't wait for it to happen. What the verse says: you have to make it happen and not wait for life, someone, an entity, your mother, your boss, your boyfriend, to make it happen.

In general, the greatest achievements, the most remarkable events, those moments we never forget, are the result of personal initiative. It's very rare that something great and important just falls into your lap. So you have to go for it. And if that means offering yourself, so be it.

If you have a passive attitude to life, it's unlikely that anyone will guess your abilities and give you a job, invite you to do business, find out what you think or see you as a great lover and companion and offer to date you.

Many things I've achieved in my life have been the result of my ability to offer. Many years ago, I went to Santa Casa in Porto Alegre and offered to the medical director to develop an outpatient service focused on mood disorders. Around 1990, we created the Santa Casa Affective Disorders Service (SEDA). At the time, there was no emphasis on this type of illness. It was a pioneering initiative, emphasizing the diagnosis and treatment of depression, which was little known and talked about at the time.

Of course, it doesn't always work. But we'll only know if we try. Even if it doesn't work out, then we have a positive opportunity, a chance to build up a "shell", to become more resilient to the hardships of life - as well as knowing which paths not to take when we want a certain thing. There are few things in life that don't have at least some favorable aspect, even if the whole seems largely negative.

So it's about taking an active, propositional stance. But not aggressively. If you're interested in someone, don't expect them to take the initiative. If you want a job, maybe it's not enough just to send in your CV, but don't come in and say that you're going to revolutionize the company or anything like that. Don't offer what you can't deliver. Offer yourself, present your skills, make it clear what you want and what you can offer.

Be clear, be direct. For everything. Even to make it clear what you're not capable of. As in the case of employment. It's no good promising the world and then failing to deliver on a day-to-day basis. Emphasize your qualities and possibilities, but also make it clear what you're not comfortable with or simply aren't qualified to do.

It's important to highlight other forms of offering, in which a more humanistic character predominates. Helping with household chores, looking after your room, your clothes, the space you share with others, washing the dishes without being asked, carrying something heavier for a frail person, paying attention to someone looking for information, answering emails, etc. Realize that offering is fundamental if we are to pave the way for greater participation and acceptance.

The question we should ask ourselves is this: **Why is it so difficult to go after what we want, what we desire?** What's more, why don't we offer to help someone? Why don't we get close to someone we're interested in and start a conversation? There will be no shortage of explanations for our obstacles. We'll have plenty of excuses, real or imagined. "*I'm shy...*" is the most common one. "*I'm not a show-off*" is also recurrent.

Imagine yourself going to a party to meet someone. When you get there, you look around and see the scene. You try to identify if someone is flirting with you. What do you do with the flirt? Strike up a conversation? Wait for them to come to you? Even without flirting, if you're interested in someone, "pay to see", try to approach them. Confront them, introduce yourself, say you're nervous, afraid, but go. You might say: "*But what if they give me the cold shoulder?*". It doesn't matter, just do your bit, that's enough.

I understand the fear of receiving a **NO**. But worse than receiving a "no" is receiving nothing at all, for not having taken any action. Please don't fill your face with swill to get up the courage. This also applies to other drugs. If you go down this path of seeking courage with drugs, you will always use this trick, and the result will be disastrous. In these cases, it wasn't your initiative, it was alcohol's (or the other drug's).

Perhaps what makes the most sense of our lack of ability to offer ourselves is our inner world, our psyche. Everyone wants to be liked, loved, considered, applauded and recognized. OK! We evaluate the external world, what surrounds us, people, what we hear, based on our observation, perception and feelings. If we have a tendency to disqualify ourselves, diminish ourselves, think we're less than others, it becomes difficult to make contacts, to get close to people. Does that make sense to you?

What is self-esteem? It's the way we evaluate ourselves. How much we think we are worth in the eyes of others and in our own eyes. We can have high self-esteem or low self-esteem. Low self-esteem is the big problem and much more common. It doesn't matter if other people think we're cool, competent or liked, because it's our own evaluation that weighs us down. Why do we belittle ourselves, put ourselves down so much? Perhaps the most important origin of this feeling of worthlessness has to do with our childhood relationships, with how we were treated by our parents or caregivers. It's common for parents to belittle children and even physically abuse them, for couples to fight, for children to go through all sorts of deprivations and abuses.

Another reason for not offering oneself has to do with a feeling of grandiosity or omnipotence. People with these personality traits think they are very special and important, and can't tolerate not being accepted in their initiatives and desires. Nobody is special, even the most beautiful, rich and powerful. We are all the same inside, with our fears and our weaknesses. So offer yourself. But remember: don't get upset if the recipient of your offer says "no". Be open to everything - to success and failure. That's life. But never, never hide. Waiting - definitely - is not knowing.

Hope is an attitude or desire that something will happen, but without our direct participation. People often place their expectations in God: "I have divine hope; I give myself into God's hands." I'm not criticizing anyone's faith or religiosity, but before asking God, look within yourself for the strength, energy and determination to overcome the difficulties that life imposes. Don't forget this passage from the Bible: "Jesus said, "Help yourself, and I will help you." Offering ourselves is the equivalent of asking for help in the face of our difficulties.

* * *

In conclusion: please realize that writing this book is an act of offering on my part. The book may be accepted or not, it may be successful or not. The result of our offering is not the primary or fundamental thing, but what matters is our movement in search of something that interests us or that we believe in.

THE TRANSGRESSIVE SIDE OF EACH OF US

Human beings are a naturally aggressive species and try not to comply with the norms inherent in the group to which they belong. To do this, they will seek consent and authorization, both in the internal (or psychic) world and in the external sphere. Everyone's so-called conscience is very permeable, flexible, venal and corruptible. This is definitely not a "nice" being, full of love and peace to offer.

Aggressiveness is an inherent characteristic in all of us. Without exception. We are potentially transgressive, aggressive, violent and dangerous. It can be a bit frightening to read this, to come face to face with the fact that everyone has a little monster inside them. Don't be alarmed, because culture, education, morals and laws help us to develop this pernicious side of humans. But it would be even more risky not to know how to recognize and deal with these aggressive impulses. (Of course, we will also need a certain amount of aggression in life's situations, so we can't live without this impulsive source).

The other day, in an interview for a local radio station, the presenter was impressed by the attitude of a doctor: in a traffic dispute, he got out of his car with a baseball bat and hit the side of another car. The journalist asked me what kind of disorder this colleague must have. I replied that such is the nature of human beings, susceptible to these reactions, and that perhaps the guy didn't have a mental disorder. (I then thought that **perhaps** disarmament would make sense at a time like this. It could be a revolver instead of a baseball bat in the hand of the aggressor. This difference in the type of instrument could lead to the death of the other).

For some people, perceiving themselves as aggressive can generate a lot of discomfort and upset, as if these impulses were demonic. We can develop inner psychic mechanisms to deny and repress these feelings and become quiet, overly cordial, passive, inert and conformist. Afraid of exploding, we start to act in a way that could lead to implosion, to bursting from the inside out. Also, in this matter of aggression, always trying to repress it can lead to other adverse reactions.

Let's enrich the text with a few examples. A person is very angry and tries to contain himself and not let his anger show, but in the end he develops a high blood pressure crisis. Some people often faint as an unconscious way of containing their anger, because the fear of losing control and doing something bad is too great.

Another common situation is when a person starts to cry in the face of a very irritating situation. It works as an attempt to protect themselves, where the emotional response comes through crying, to get the aggressive impulse out of the way. How many of us start to stutter when we're very angry? It's a way of stopping words or swear words from coming out, perhaps very forceful and aggressive. And there are many other examples.

The use of alcohol or other drugs is a risk factor that can break the subject's internal control over aggressive feelings. In minor situations, such as a banal argument between neighbors or about soccer teams, it can have serious consequences, such as murdering someone. Alcohol is a potentiator of aggression and transgression, reducing the internal repression of these impulses. Look at the damage drunk drivers cause!

Of course, I'm not here suggesting measures and ways or manuals to appear nice and well-behaved. Personally, I always keep an eye on my feelings and reactions. I don't like who I become when I take intemperate actions, with my anger coming out in an exaggerated way.

Look at another way of acting that is very present in people: **transgression**. It's a strong word, referring to acts of great evil. Robbing a bank, beating someone up, corrupting yourself... All this is transgression. But that's not all. There are countless small acts that fall into this category. Cutting in line, running a red light, not respecting a crosswalk, talking on a cell phone while driving, small lies, not returning a borrowed book... These are the most common examples of transgressions. I don't mean to be moralistic, but I just want to point out that these attitudes also occur on a daily basis among so-called good people.

* * *

Let's do an exercise. We can all transgress at times, but what really differentiates us from a great transgressor, or an outcast?

In the small transgressions of everyday life, we reach the edge of the precipice and return. The marginal, the outlaw, the bandit, passes that margin of safety and throws himself over the precipice, not returning to the space of normality. He tries to parachute into the gorge, wanting to land on his feet and without trauma. But he can't.

This explains the corrupt behavior of many politicians. In addition to making money from corruption, they don't stop this process because it brings a certain "cheapness", a "crack", a certain well-being in trying to make fools of others. (Currently, in Brazil, some politicians have thrown themselves over the cliff and the parachute hasn't opened, thanks to the intervention of that task force called Lava Jato).

Look at our most representative sport, soccer. It's full of transgressions, perpetrated by everyone from managers to players. The manager sells an athlete and earns an "edge" on the side. A player fakes an assault that didn't happen and isn't penalized for it. The other uses his hand to pull, to score a goal. And we, the fans, are not outraged by all this when it favors our team. So we are complicit and go along with the offenders.

That's us! It's hard to expect other transgressors to change their attitudes with some supernatural force. If any change in these attitudes is to come, it will depend on a different attitude on the part of the majority of the population. Perhaps the biggest factors for change will come through education, a reduction in poverty, more jobs and legislation that can be enforced quickly.

* * *

Of course, many people don't, and we can live a lifetime without getting into trouble with the law. But the transgressive impulses are always there, tempting us all the time.

WHY DO WE COMPLAIN SO MUCH?

When I was 13, I lost my father. He was a successful industrialist. I had plans to work with him. From that moment on, I was very shaken, with after-effects, as if I had to walk with the support of a crutch. Life became heavy, it seemed that nothing made sense anymore. I complained, I complained, I tended to be unhappy with the world. Always with the justification of having lost my father.

At any age, it's very sad to lose someone you love so much - let alone a teenager. However, neither that nor any other setback is enough to permanently damage your life. Fortunately, I realized this and moved on, managing not to get trapped in the grief that was becoming permanent.

It never crossed my mother's mind that I needed help; nor did I identify that I wasn't well. This is a common pattern in the lives of people who are suffering from mental illness: not realizing that they need help.

For the most diverse reasons - all of them quite reasonable - we are often complaining. Whether it's because of a major trauma or everyday issues, we complain all the time. At home, in traffic, at work and even at play. We even complain constantly about things that are beyond our control: about a corrupt politician, the inept coach of our soccer team, the attitude of an artist we admire, friends who don't call, a neighbor who has a different way of living, etc. In short, complaining is common to human beings; let's say, it's part of life.

Life is complicated and conflictual. However, faced with this realization, we only have two alternatives: either we turn life into an eternal wall of lamentation, or we learn to deal with situations - understanding them in order to absorb them and make the best of them, not conforming to the extent necessary to resolve them; and conforming to the extent necessary to avoid indulging in innocuous whining. We need to deal with life as it presents itself. It is neither fair nor unfair - it just is.

The great risk of complaining is that we turn our backs on life. It would be like driving a car backwards, looking in the rearview mirror, looking back at what has already happened. Freud coined the word **neurosis**, which describes the attitude of being attached to the past and putting all your unhappiness into it. Those who live in regret end up behaving like a poor person, a real victim of existence. In this way, they no longer take responsibility for what happens to them, nor do they feel responsible for what happens to others as a result of their inertia. After all, living is too hard for them. They therefore think that "there's simply nothing to do".

I repeat: in general, these regrets have a ring of truth to them, they are not mere inventions. Imagine a poor person who has to work a lot, so that they have very little time to spend with their children, to help them with their studies, to educate them. Imagine their frustration. However, even this unfortunate person cannot indulge in endless lamentation, otherwise they will make their life even worse and lose everything they have left that is good.

How many fathers can afford to spend time with their children and neglect to do so? Well, this father who works from sun up to sun down must be determined to make the most of every minute he has left. His life will certainly be much more satisfying than that of many people.

Speaking of social class, here's something I see all the time: people with high economic and financial status whining a lot. Money is not a vaccine against whining, boredom and annoyance. Wealthy people sometimes lead very unhappy lives because they imagine that with their money, cars, trips and everything else they will be loved and admired. Money is no substitute for affection, care, love and attention.

In short, there's never a shortage of reasons to complain. And, as I said, the reasons may even be real, but we try to turbo-charge them in our minds. The danger is that we can incorporate this pattern of functioning and become bored, irritable, dejected and discouraged with life. Complaining usually has an unconscious function, which goes unnoticed by the complainer. It's a way of not being charged or demanded by those around us. It's as if the person wants others not to expect too much from them, from the point of view of giving affection, attention, cuddles and care or even being willing to have sex, because they are someone *so needy*, for whom life has been a stepmother - "Poor me, don't ask me for anything...".

Other interesting aspects of the complainant's life. The group around them will tend to move away from them, as being around them becomes a heavy and unpleasant experience. Another possibility is that they provoke a feeling of irritation in their peers, leading to verbal abuse.

Complaining is an unconscious exercise in trying to get rid of the anxieties, annoyances and difficulties that life imposes. The chronic complainer is likely to be depressed, because the act of complaining generates negative energy in the subject. They acquire a repetitive and cumulative style of relating. Even if he starts to talk about something he thinks is good, the cackle of complaining quickly comes to mind. It's like the person who complains even in positive situations: "You know what? I won the lottery! But the worst thing is that I'm going to have to pay more taxes"; "I bought this new car, but I'm afraid to leave because of *the neighbors' big eyes*"; "I won this car, but I'm going to have more expenses now"; "My mother-in-law gave me this TV, but now she's going to want something in return".

If you suspect that you may be a complainer, ask someone close to you with whom you can be frank whether your conversation is boring, repetitive and full of bitterness. If so, ask them to point out in their daily life whether your conversation is going that way. The healthiest thing, however, is that we can develop the ability to perceive ourselves, without others having to demonstrate that our company is boring and tedious.

One reason why we complain so much is that we may not face up to the situations in which life requires us to intervene. It can be an unconscious alibi for not focusing on solving difficulties. Also, through complaining, we can expect someone to come and take care of our lives. Something like: "If life hasn't been generous to me, I owe it." We often complain about our parents because of situations in which they may have failed us, or even treated us badly.

Of course, it's up to us to resolve these issues internally, because the past has passed - and clinging to it is unhealthy.

WHEN SEX BECOMES AN ADDICTION

Addiction, dependence, vice. Its most common manifestations are related to gambling, medicines and drugs. Gambling, cards, dice. Tranquilizers, weight loss drugs, psychostimulants, alcohol, cocaine, *crack*. However, I realize that there is another addiction, one that is considerably more frequent, quieter, more discreet and less talked about: sexual addiction.

I've noticed how much people cheat on each other, married or single. Men often use an unsubstantiated maxim to justify their cheating: "I'm too horny...". Surveys are published in the media - without any scientific basis - asking how often Americans, Brazilians and Argentinians have sex; or gauchos, cariocas, paulistas and baianos. These surveys suggest that normal people have to have sex so many times a week. For many men, it seems that sex works as a competition, in the sense of seeing who has the most sex. There's a *male* saying: "Sex not given is sex lost, you can't get it back."

The main characteristic of addiction is the addict's lack of control over the object of his addiction. They no longer choose what they do, as they become hostages to this dependency. In general, this is not a state that is reached suddenly and abruptly. The path is gradual. That's why, for some people, the issue of sex can become complicated, as it becomes the main source of their pleasure. Behind this frenetic rhythm of non-stop sex can lurk a dependency or addiction to sex.

Alcohol is often the main palliative and a form of escape from life's afflictions. But some people turn to sex. And this is more common among men than women. They look to sex as an escape valve for unconscious psychological anxieties and emptiness. Initially, they may not be addicted to sex, but as time goes by, they realize that sex temporarily relieves that subjective malaise. The reader might ask: "Better addicted to sex than drugs, right?" Great question! Answer: it's best not to be addicted to **anything**!

If you suspect that you're going through this, there's an almost foolproof way to be sure. If, after the sex you went for with the intention of relieving tension, you feel a bit melancholy, depressed, with something like an emptiness inside, you probably fit the case I'm talking about here. It's very possible that you're developing this addiction.

And the mechanism is the same as with drugs: after the euphoria comes the emptiness. What then? The addict's response is to seek new doses of what he's addicted to. They go in search of a new partner, establish yet another superficial relationship, get that brief release from their afflictions and then find themselves forced to start the cycle of their addiction all over again.

I've heard terrible confessions from men in this condition that, after sex, if they could, they would get rid of their partner at any cost. "If I could, I'd put her in a cab..."; "I wish I could press a button to eject her from my bed". Cruelty, no? However, above the real contempt for the woman, there is the manifestation of the emptiness that the subject feels as a result of casual sex, of the dose that he has consumed as a result of his addiction. Absolutely degrading.

It's important to say that this type of addiction doesn't depend on the addict's regular sex life. I mean, it's common for me to come across patients who love their partner, who are satisfied with the sexual relations they have at home, but who nevertheless can't stop *venturing out*, looking for sex on the street.

Notice how the lack of control has taken over this person's life. Addictions are powerful mechanisms for entangling us in the **art of being unhappy**. Imagine that there are people who have access at home to what they are addicted to, but who take risks with strangers in the search for more and more. Absolutely sick!

The opposite of vices are virtues. Coming from a religious background, virtues are not, contrary to popular belief, the annulment of the pleasures of vices. Rather, they are the subject's control over himself, dosing and taming what pleases him.

If his vice is anger, which makes him go berserk against apparent injustices, it doesn't mean that he should stop reacting; rather, he should resort to the virtue of meekness, so that he learns to keep calm and analyze situations coldly, realizing if they are in fact unjust, before reacting with the necessary force. If his addiction is to sex, to lust, this means that he values what is beautiful and pleasurable; so let him seek out other beautiful and pleasurable things in life - the company and even sex with his loved one, spending time with friends, good food, in short, things that won't leave him empty after a brief peak of euphoria.

* * *

What is striking is that these habitual addicts need to use Viagra during these encounters. As the response to Viagra is not satisfactory, they use between 1 and 3 pills to get an erection. This is a clear indicator that they are experiencing unattractive relationships, because they have a dissociation between the genuine desire to have sex and the compulsion to do so. Of course, there are also health risks from taking too much Viagra. Many men have died in motels.

THE HARM OF CULTIVATING REVENGE

"An eye for an eye, a tooth for a tooth." Who hasn't heard this phrase? It dates back to 1780 B.C. and is found in the Law of Talion, in the Code of Hammurabi, a set of laws written in Mesopotamia, the oldest in humanity, which authorized revenge, "he who strikes with iron shall be struck with iron".

If there's one strong feeling that promises to be satisfyingly rewarding, it's the desire for revenge. But stronger than its promises are its harmful consequences.

I'm going to propose a practical division so that we can better understand the feeling of revenge. There are two types of revenge: conscious and unconscious. Both are very bad for our mental health and even our physical well-being. They can cause gastritis, raise blood pressure, lead to loss of sleep, generate permanent anxiety and much more. These are feelings that take over our being, control our moods and drive our actions. In other words, it doesn't matter whether the intention to take revenge is an indomitable impulse or a rational plan; either way, it's something that intoxicates us. It's a kind of impulse that enslaves us.

The desire for conscious revenge is easy to identify and doesn't need much explanation. It's something that arises and is perceived by the person, who then acts to carry out their plan. However, when this feeling is unconscious, it becomes even more dangerous, even though it is just as malevolent.

It's important to reflect and understand the repercussions on our emotions of everyday situations in which we feel unqualified and mistreated. For some people, feeling angry is almost unacceptable, because they don't know how to accommodate this feeling within themselves. They fear losing control and letting this anger spill over into an explosive situation, attacking or hitting the other person. In this way, in an attempt to control themselves, they can turn the impulse into depression, discouragement and a loss of ability to carry on with their tasks or enjoy their daily lives. It is not possible to store this harmful and even toxic feeling that is repressed anger, because it will spill out at some point. This is the ideal breeding ground for the emergence of unconscious revenge, which leads to an unthinking attack on the aggressor, but also on oneself, as it causes the person to lose a lot of energy.

A good example to illustrate how unconscious revenge occurs is in working relationships. Think of an embarrassing situation in which a boss is dismissive, scornful or rude to an employee. The employee is - shall we say - hierarchically prevented from reacting appropriately. The subordinate will hardly have enough freedom to respond in the proper way to the superior who has treated him in a rude, vexatious manner. So he tries to *swallow the frog* immediately. However, the toad doesn't allow itself to be digested, it always remains stuck in the throat. Even if he tries to forget the hurt, the worker tends to hold a grudge. And that's when unconscious revenge arises.

Without realizing it, the embarrassed employee then begins to sabotage his own work, loses the desire and energy to work, is slow to meet targets, is late and delivers poorly executed tasks. Of course, at the end of the day, it is the employer who will be the loser, as he will end up suffering some financial loss as a result of his employee's vindictive incompetence. However, it is unlikely that the boss will not foot the bill for his unconscious revenge. Of course, the functioning described above will consume the subject's energy, bring psychological discomfort and, as a result, the presence of symptoms such as anguish, irritability, apathy, etc. Another possible damage could be dismissal.

Another example: a woman who is upset with her husband, but can't talk about her annoyances. She is asked to have sex every night. She gives in, but it doesn't feel good and she ends up not enjoying it. If she expresses her dissatisfaction with sex, she fears that her husband might look for another, hotter partner. Get on with it! Soon, she may feel pain during sex, which will allow her to withdraw from sex, as if she wasn't the one who decided not to have sex anymore. It's a surreptitious boycott.

It's also common to see this kind of *under-the-table banter* with a partner in male sexuality. As a result of conflicts or discontent between the couple, which have not been properly discussed and overcome, an unexpected premature ejaculation can occur at the height of sex. It's unconscious revenge that comes into play. Bad for both of you.

What a head we have, eh?

More. Imagine a family environment full of annoyances due to the attitudes and words of relatives. Trying to maintain an unfeasible harmony, with good manners, we submit, silently putting up with the disrespect. Suddenly, however, we may feel unwell in that environment and, because of some physical or mental discomfort, we may have an anxiety attack or an upset stomach. It will be an authorization that we build to withdraw. Another stealthy action of our imagination.

I remember a friend who told me the following: his wife was traveling and he was going to pick her up at the airport. The relationship wasn't going well; he reported that his wife was very bossy and he tended to submit. When he arrived, he went off to do other chores and ended up forgetting about his wife. He asked me if he needed to take some medication for his memory. Since I knew the story of the two of them, I thought it was funny and said that perhaps the forgetfulness signaled a wish that she hadn't come back. Another unconscious revenge.

Another guy was angry with his wife, who had entered the menopause and lost the desire to have sex. Today, medicine doesn't recommend hormone replacement, so women tend to lose libido and have little vaginal lubrication during this period. This is a disadvantage for women, as men don't experience this situation. Even though he knew about this physiological situation, he remained upset and wanted to take revenge by having sex with another woman. I realized that he experienced this as if it were his wife's way of screwing with him.

Look at the situation of a man who was cheated on by his girlfriend and who was very upset and depressed by the fact. He became obsessed with making her suffer, on the basis of the Law of Talion. Of course, he's not responsible for the betrayal, it was his girlfriend's decision. As time goes by and he keeps coming up with plans to harm the girl, his life becomes stagnant, stuck with his ex-girlfriend, revealing how paralyzed and psychologically ill he is. If he only got upset, if he only got depressed, the resolution of this grief would be quicker and healthier. Revenge is related to the idea of remaining attached to the other - and by imposing pain on them, it confirms their imprisonment.

Even if we do something harmful to the other person, we'll wonder if the damage has been done to them, and so we'll remain fixated on this endless rumination. To keep revenge alive, we need to feed it with anger and the desire for retaliation. These two components attack us internally, as if we were drinking glasses of acid every day. It's a terrible business that can only be justified by our poor mental health and our desire to control the other person.

It's good to keep in mind these unpleasant situations in life, to know that, yes, people - sooner or later - will displease us, annoy us, hurt us. And we will also do this to others. We are imperfect beings - or rather, clumsy, limited, *ordinary*.

It's possible to say that those who want revenge want to be tied to the other person; they don't want to resolve the hurt. There's a saying: "Better alone than in bad company." For the person who wants revenge, the saying is reversed: "Better unaccompanied than alone", because the other person is still present in their imagination, in their day-to-day life.

To reiterate: the avenger takes revenge on himself, because he is paralyzed and uncommitted to taking care of his life. Their energy is fixed on this unhealthy process, which borders on psychosis. Thought never leaves this rumination. It's like an old vinyl record with the needle locked, making the music repeat itself. It's maddening!

We can think of some antidotes to reduce the risk of revenge. This means accepting that we are not so important and wonderful in the eyes of life and others; expressing through words our annoyance at something we don't like; revealing to the abuser our disagreement with their attitude; not feeling wronged by life's setbacks; between taking revenge or withdrawing from a relationship, preferring the latter; being clear that we can be betrayed, even if we don't do anything about it; knowing that life is neither fair nor unfair. **Life just is**.

ABOUT THE AUTHOR

Graduated in Medicine from the Federal University of Rio Grande do Sul in 1972, Nelio Tombini did his residency in general surgery at the Hospital de Clínicas in Porto Alegre, before working for three years as a surgeon, clinician, obstetrician and anesthesiologist in the interior of Rio Grande do Sul, in Guarani das Missões.

Back in the capital, he specialized in psychiatry and began the career summarized in this book. He worked as a psychiatrist in health centers, the São José do Murialdo Community Center, the Judicial Asylum, the São Pedro Hospital and the Spiritist Psychiatric Hospital.

In 1990, he created the Affective Diseases Service at Santa Casa de Porto Alegre, where he was responsible for the psychiatric sector for 22 years, developing a group psychotherapy project for patients in the public health system.

Nelio Tombini is the founder and director of Psicobreve - Clínica de Psicoterapia Breve. Currently, through lectures, workshops, business consultancies and the online video series *5 minutes with psychiatrist Nelio Tombini,* he is developing a psycho-educational project for the general public. He also continues to work as a psychiatrist and psychotherapist.

Facebook: facebook.com/drneliotombini

YouTube: youtube.com/Psicobreve

Instagram: instagram.com/drneliotombini

CITADEL
Grupo Editorial